LEAD , KINDLY LIGHT

Edmund Preston

Published and Printed January 2004
© January 2004 Elizabeth Preston

ISBN 0952769468

FOREWORD

Edmund Preston - Dedications

For more than 40 years, my friend Edmund Preston and I have shared a journey of spiritual education and growth, through the teachings we received from the founder and leader of the Spiritualist Church - 'A Temple of the Trinity' in North London, Mrs Eva Rayner with her spirit control, Dr. Thomas Lewis. We both developed our mediumship, which has given us practical awareness of the reality of eternal life, the significance of reincarnation and the purpose of our lives on earth. We shared a great love for the Master Jesus, reverencing the example his life provides, and the spiritual content of his teachings. For many years, we both have carried forward these truths by leading weekly study groups and conducting regular Sunday services. Edmund was the medium for a spirit teacher called Brother Peter, who used him to give inspiring and revealing Biblical interpretation, by looking beyond the word to reveal the true spirit. He gave the listener a greater awareness of Divine Purpose, God's justice, the Christ Love and mankind's growth through experience and pain. His legacy in this book expresses his spiritual insight and the realisation that our present understanding is only at the beginning of the great journey of discovery, finding one's true self and that essence of God within. He too, fully realised that to begin to learn, you must have an open mind.

Michael Bull
President.   'A Temple of the Trinity Lodge for Spiritual Healing'

Edmund was also very interested in spiritual/religious experience and was a regular attendee at the meetings of the Alister Hardy Society in London. He enjoyed and participated in the Society's London Group lectures and discussions, quietly sharing his insights, which were considerable.

John Franklin
The Alister Hardy Society.

{ The Alister Hardy Society supports the work of the Religious Experience Research Centre studying contemporary spiritual/religious experience at the University of Wales, Lampeter }
www.alisterhardytrust.org.uk

Edmund was a very enthusiastic disciple of Pierre Teilhard de Chardin, the Jesuit Palaeontologist, whose perceptions of the evolutionary process and spirituality are reflected in these essays. Edmund was a member of the British Teilhard Association for many years and regularly attended the annual conferences.

Barbara Hogg
The British Teilhard Association.

ACKNOWLEDGEMENTS

Peter Cox and Barbara Hogg - Members of the British Teilhard Association for their time and encouragement in promoting this book.

Elaine Hall-Freeman and Anni Butler for their help and computer knowledge.

Glynne Thomas for his kindness in offering to proof read the articles.

Karen Ardouin for all her help and support.

Kim Cross for his time, advice and computer skills - without which this book would not have been published.

Contents

Fuchsia

1. SPIRITUAL LEADERSHIP

What are the lessons that all true leaders have to learn? Let us briefly look at one or two so that we can begin to master them, to understand their need, and to apply them to our lives with a view of achieving a fuller and more useful life.

The first lesson is the lesson of vision. What are our goals? What is the spiritual incentive which will be strong enough to hold us steady to the purpose and remain true to our objectives? No one can formulate the vision for us; it is our own personality problem, and how much we achieve and become will depend upon the strength of the vision and the beauty of the picture which we paint with our imagination.

The second lesson is the development of a right sense of proportion. This, when properly developed, will enable us to walk with humility, for we then realise the magnitude of the task, and appreciate the limitations of our contribution in the light of our own vision. The need, therefore, is constant self-development, and the cultivation of steady inner spiritual learning. We help others through our own efforts to attain this. This means clearer thinking, humility and constant adjustment.

The third lesson is the development and appreciation of the underlying unity of all life in all its forms. This enables us to include all within the range of our influence, and that means also those greater than ourselves. Thus, a chain of contacts is established upwards towards the one great whole we call God.

Another lesson which grows out of the previous one is the avoidance of the spirit of criticism for that creates barriers and so wastes valuable time. We must learn to distinguish between the spirit of criticism and the ability to analyse and make practical suggestion or approach. Learn to analyse life, circumstances, and people from the angle of the work needed, and not from the point of view of ones personality.

Leaders have to learn to stand alone, and they can do so only if they love enough.

2.   GUIDING PRINCIPLES

The present era of transition between an old order and a new one can be described as the age of anxiety. I'd rather call it an age of anxiety than an age of fear, in spite of the extreme fear so prevalent in many areas of the world, for anxiety is global , stemming from the uncertainty in world conditions both politically and economically.

To this great confusion must be added the loss by mankind of any guiding concept of either a religious or a philosophical nature that might give any acceptable meaning for life itself. The strain of constructing a meaningful life is stimulating and healthy, but the strain of fear, futility and injustice, with no acceptable reason for living is spiritual misery.

There is a need for a new vision to appear strongly enough so that people will pay attention to it. But without any standard of values worth living for, how can this vision impinge upon human minds effectively? Can any influence be observed flowing within our midst which is capable of inspiring people into believing in a concept of values, which goes beyond mere physical comforts and possessions? We are all groping for these answers consciously or unconsciously. There are, however, some glimpses of deeper truths emerging as mankind is reaching towards new standards. This quest must be intelligently pursued with open mindedness and freedom from prejudice.

There are some potent concepts which are so fundamental to human welfare that a careful consideration of them must bring a renewed faith in the ultimate destiny of mankind. As suggestive of these concepts it might be possible to list certain ideas:-

1) There is a God: this basic idea cannot be crushed out of human thought as it is inherent in the fact of existence.
2) This God is good: to conceive that an intelligent cause of all that is could be evil is as fantastic as to believe that it is all a matter of chance. Then if God is good, the fulfilment of what He has visioned and set in motion is absolutely assured. In this we all participate.
3) There is a plan for mankind: if we acknowledge that there is no question of chance in the mind of God, then there must be a reason for his creation. There must be a reason why there is such a thing as humanity on this planet, and if there is a plan, there must be a way of bringing it about.
4) This plan for mankind is Good: if there is a God, and he is a good God, and he has a plan, then that plan must be good. Now if it is good, then it is worth every effort to understand it. If we could see the necessity for the existence of such a plan and set ourselves to learn of its operations so as

to conform with it, then surely rapid progress would be made towards world peace and a better way of life.

5) Evolution is the unfolding of this plan in time and consciousness: men are not robots or slaves to the forces that surround them. Humanity must increasingly handle its own evolution and work out its own destiny. That destiny must be in terms of spiritual values and not, as at present, in terms of material possessions and comforts.

6) This plan is being implemented among men, by those higher spiritual beings who know more of God's plan than those of us who have never stopped to consider or attempt to find out about it. Such people do exist. The facts of a plan and of these greater spiritual lives need to be understood by men for stabilization in the present era of anxiety and fear. For when men realise that God's purpose is being worked out for the welfare of humanity, then their focus of attention must turn away from self-centred desires but towards those desires for the welfare of all humanity, so becoming more in tune with the thinking of those spiritual beings who are the custodians of God's plans. Thus it is that men become more useful spiritually.

3. MEDIATORS BETWEEN GOD AND MAN

Right down the ages, and in every country, times of tension and distress have always brought with them some hopeful sense of expectancy. For it seems that when men feel that they have exhausted all their innate possibilities and that the problems and conditions confronting them are beyond their solving or handling, then they are apt to look for some divine mediator who can come and bring about a rescue. This thought of a divine mediator between God and man (A Messiah) can be found running like a golden thread through all the world faiths, and indeed we do know that great and divine representatives of God the Father have come from time to time, and have always left a changed world. This surely expresses two basic incentives: the need for God to be in constant contact with mankind, and the need of mankind for continuous divine help and understanding

These mediators are of all degrees and kinds. They all express within themselves some future development, and they strike a note or expound a teaching which can bring in a new time cycle, a new civilisation, or a new age. They all have that great gift of having those spiritual qualities which the people around them can recognise as truths that are worth striving and working for.

The two teachers mostly easily known and recognised are the Buddha in the East, and the Christ in the West. Their messages are familiar to a great number, and the fruits of their lives and words have conditioned the thinking and civilisations of both hemispheres. Because they were so humanly divine, they have come to be trusted and loved by millions. The centres of spiritual energy which each of them set up is beyond measure, and it is the establishing of a centre of persistent spirit power that is the constant task of any who would act as a divine mediator between God and man. This would set up a focal point in the world of human living in order to transmit spiritual powers and forces that would enable mankind to express some divine idea which in time would produce a civilisation with all its accompanying culture, religions, governments, and educational processes. Thus is history made. History after all is the record of humanity's reaction to some divine leader or leaders.

Until the Christ came and lived a life of love and service, and giving the new commandment to love one another, there had been very little emphasis upon God as Love in any of the world scriptures. After He had come and lived as the embodiment of love, then God became known as Love. Love became the basic principle of all relationships. This divine quality was revealed and emphasised by Christ, thus altering all human goals and values for living.

Today, there is this great need to develop a spiritual recognition in order to restore man's faith in the Father's Love and in the way of life that the Christ taught. Mankind stands between an unhappy past and a future which is full of promise, and looks once more for some divine mediator or medium of the Great Spirit to sound that note, and give that teaching that can bring in the beginnings of a new era.

4.   CHANGE

It is very easy to become satisfied and to arrive at a 'self-containment' so comfortable that anything tending to disturb it is viewed with dismay and. distrust. This attitude spells the death of progress, for livingness demands movement, and to grow spiritually there must be a constant ebb and flow between creation and destruction.

Now because this living movement involves pain and demands adjustment, men tend to put off the experience. They close their minds to any new ideas, seeking by all means possible to maintain the security of their normal thought patterns. This has been, and still is, the main dragging force which holds seekers of the spiritual life from the growth which they should be demonstrating in their lives. If there is one word which would describe today's world, that word is "Change". It is apparent in every aspect of life. The "Old" look at the way the young people live and are appalled. The "Young" look at their elders and are frightened by the lack of elasticity in their outlook. Yet these are all men and women who are working for basically common objectives, blessed by common joys and harassed by common anxieties. Surely it would need only a small change in the outlook of both to melt down the hard edges of divergence, and so draw all to a centre from whence unified action could be taken and a more universal outlook achieved.

It is said that when a master of the spirit seeks to work through a student of the spirit life, he faces a big difficulty in bringing to an end the period of intense self-preoccupation that the student has in how he is doing in his service and with his own ideas and interpretations of what is true. When, as is now-a-days more usual, the work is with a group of students, the difficulty is even greater, for now the master has to deal with a group of people with their fixed ideas all of which they are sure are entirely correct, and who hold the conviction that they have reached a point in their development where they have registered certain spiritual values. The first thing then that the master has to do, if true spiritual work is to emerge, is to blast the group wide open and give its members a deep sense of insecurity. This prepares them for the reception of newer and deeper approaches to truth. Movement of all and in everything is the very basis of existence, and so one needs to learn to love change not so much the external as the internal. Such as one's attitude of mind, emotion, and of the spirit. Sadly, in so many spiritual groupings, this love of change is lacking, as their members cling to their certainties and to what they have achieved.

One must always remember that truth : that enduring intangible flame of the spirit, in some way changes whomsoever it touches and it is this change that is the root cause of the non—ease or discomfiture which is produced whenever new ideas, a new vision, new relationships, and new values rise up to challenge accepted and established presentations of truth, or rather those human interpretations of what is true. Far too many spiritual students want to be right more than they want to discover the real depths of the spirit. Awakening to the truth of the spirit does not happen only once, but again and again. The worth of any spiritual group lies in its eagerness to awaken again and yet again to new vistas and more a extended vision.

Throughout the ages the New has challenged the Old. Challenged, but not always replaced. New approaches are not necessarily better than those worn smooth by pioneering minds, but they do present fresh opportunities for a rethink. The importance of new approaches lies in their power to break up thought patterns that have become too firmly established, so giving new glimpses of the fragments of eternal truth which is all men ever achieve. Discomforting influences deserve welcome; dissenting statements should be hailed with joy, irrespective of the temporary inconvenience they create; for these are the means of renewal. Spiritual living does not call for comfort, security or continuance; on the contrary, it demands a constant willingness to change, an eagerness to alter and modify forms, no matter how loved or sustaining these have become. All this is necessary in order that the indwelling life may come into a fuller expression. Thus it will be found possible to see and welcome new approaches to truth which produce pain, only because they also produce LIFE.

5.   THE WORD "SPIRITUAL"

The word "Spiritual" does not refer to any so called religious matters but relates to experience to another. It relates to the moving forward from one level of consciousness, no matter how low or gross the next. When we come to realise that events, circumstances, happenings, and physical phenomena of every kind are simply the effects of what is happening in inner worlds, then we must realise that the development of the so called irreligious man into a sound and effective businessman, with all the necessary equipment for success, is as much a spiritual unfoldment in his experience as the understanding of the laws of God may be to a highly developed religious man.

The assumption by Orthodox Church people that the word "Spiritual" denotes profound and effective interest in religion is not borne out by the facts of spiritual life. Someday when the world is led by people who are under close guidance from the spirit this erroneous assumption will be discarded and it will be realised that all activity which drives the human being forward towards some development, whether physical, emotional, mental, or the spirit, is essentially spiritual in nature as it is indicative of the livingness of the inner divine spark. Therefore the discoveries of science, or the production of some great work in literature or art are just as much evidence of spiritual unfoldment as the rhapsodies of any mystic.

There does, however, come a point in the experience of those taking a spiritual. approach along their specialised lines where a meeting place will become apparent and where a common goal will be recognised, where the essential unity within the different forms and methods will be acknowledged, and where pilgrims on all the varied ways of approach will know themselves to be one band of demonstrators of the divine.

If you will note your attitudes and actions, you will discover that primarily they centre around yourselves, your grasp of truth and your own progress. But as your self-interest declines and disappears, that which remains is only of beauty, goodness, and truth. These are not words which describe any structure or form, but words which describe qualities behind the forms. This indicates the spirit behind the form and when you are expressing these qualities, you are living spiritually. At present what is called "Spiritual living" by so many is in reality an expression of themselves and the truth as they grasp it, or of nature as they scientifically interpret it. However, what the spirit may be seeking to express may not be what mankind believes needs expressing, so it is for people who acknowledge the pressure and guidance of spirit to demonstrate the true spiritual life.

Christ showed this life in himself. Inevitably what he lived coloured human thinking and so the Christian Church took form, but that form was of men expressing themselves, and imposing their interpretations of truth on Truth itself. They created a massive organisation from which 'the life' is non-existent. True Christianity will be expressed when the activity of the spirit of love flows naturally and automatically through the mediumship of groups of people such as those of you who can absorb and express in daily living the true reality behind the turmoil of life.

Therefore, there is ahead of us the life of spirit working to express what is true and good through an ever closer contact with minds and hearts open to receive. Many are being called because of their development and because of the contribution they should be able to make. That contribution expresses the true Spiritual life and intention.

6. "SPIRITUAL GROWTH"

The interpretation of the words "Spiritual growth" is usually that of growing in religious understanding. A man is deemed to be "Spiritual" if he shows an interest in the scriptures, is a member of a church, and leads a saintly life. But this cannot be a true definition for it is not sufficiently comprehensive. This is a definition that has grown out of the impression set upon human thought by a past age, and in particular by the Christian church - all most necessary in its time, but which has led to the over-emphasis of some of God's expressions and the overlooking of others just as viable of divine thought. Therefore any truer meaning of the words "Spiritual growth" must be far wider and more all-embracing than that which has come to us through the media of religious literature and organisations.

For instance we could take the words "power ","purpose", and " will" and agree that these words all describe qualities and expressions of God. Yet they may show themselves with equal clarity through a Hitler as through a Pope. In both cases the recipient receives an essentially divine quality, modifies it and steps it down according to what is in him - that is to say, according to his spiritual growth. So we see that any person may function in any walk of life and his work will warrant the description "Spiritual" just as so far as it is based on an inner guidance for what may be imagined as ideal. We see therefore, why all true spiritual teachers will place so strong an emphasis on motive. People who are strongly individual in their outlook and yet are developing a sense of the group life, must inevitably find their way into a school of the spirit where they are guided in such a manner that the nature of the soul unfolds and slowly overpowers them. This makes them increasingly sensitive to that spirit within; the qualities of that spirit are knowledge, love, and a great willingness to give of one's self in the service of others. The measure of one's spiritual growth can be taken as the measure of one's control that this spirit has over the outer life. The outstanding characteristics of those people who are not as yet soul-centred or controlled are ambition, pride, an aggressive dominance, and a lack of love towards the whole, though they frequently possess a love for those who are necessary to them or to their well-being.

The problem for each individual person consists in ascertaining upon which step of the ladder one finds oneself at any particular moment of time, for behind each human being stretches a long series of lives. So many today have just reached that stage of dominant selfishness, this for them is as much a step forward in spiritual growth from what they have been, as any who have passed beyond that stage and no longer work or play to make an impact on those around them, but who strive to lead a life of selflessness and service in a subordination to the larger whole. One who is only just learning the A.B.C. of the spiritual life with all its failures and dense stupidities may be doing as well as any other with more knowledge and experience. To those who have not yet grown to the full stature of the spirit and where the vision is not so clear, there must be the all important work of working with their kind. For them the home and the office provide the supreme opportunity for the spirit within to learn control and balance. All those that look for spiritual growth there must respond to the call to see life as it truly is, and not with its many distinctions which are man-made and therefore misleading, not to mention dangerous.

In the coming age which even now is being born, the true growth of the spirit will be carried forward only by those people who refuse to be separate in their outlook and who watch their words with care. They are those who will see only the good and divine in all things, and their lives will be coloured by an understanding and love for all things.

7.   "THE SPIRIT WITHIN"

The history of mankind is the history of the individual search for divine expression and the achievement of that something, which releases a man into the service of the kingdom of God. That kingdom exists, and to be born into it is as inescapable as being born into a human family. Through birth, service, and sacrifice you become a citizen of that kingdom, and it is as much a natural process of a spiritual life as is the physical life that people are so engrossed in. The two go together.

The way into the kingdom is found by questioning and answering; by seeking and finding, and by an obedience to that inner voice which can be heard when all other voices are stilled. For there comes a point of spiritual development when one is sufficiently sensitive to the influence of the divine so as to be aware of what one might call "God's Will" being expressed through a voice from within. When this prompting is heard then one becomes aware of the possibilities of God within ourselves, and realise in ourselves there is that outpouring of divine love that makes us appreciate that all lives are part of one great whole. Could it not be said then that we are meeting the Christ spirit within, and would not this voice and love indicate the way that we must go just as does the bible story of the Christ indicated the way - the way that leads away from the superficial and material into the world of inner reality. The Christ in his life on earth showed what man should be: to be obedient to the highest in us all, and completely confident in that power of God to demonstrate the life of loving service in practice. We have in ourselves, if we could but realise it, exactly those circumstances and the environment in which the great lesson of obedience to the highest may be learnt. For it is this which provides the tests that reveal our strengths and weaknesses. Surely God needs men and women so tested in order to meet the difficulties of a life of service to the human race, and it is this life of service that is the straight and narrow road which leads to what we call the kingdom of God, and which was so clearly demonstrated in the life of the Christ. He left us that example and we must carry on the work which he began. It is no good studying the life of the Christ from a distance and wonder at his achievements, or even to try and copy him. For surely he would not want us to copy him, but rather that we should prove to ourselves and to the world that the divinity which is in him, is in us also.

What can we do to respond to this call for holiness? Number one, it entails effort; the will to exert ourselves in overcoming the lower nature and in listening to the insistent demands of the spirit within. This calls for two great recognitions: first that presence of the spirit within which can be known through the process of daily living; and secondly, the determination to achieve a refocusing of one's entire life into a closer identification with the spirit of all things. From this one begins to assume a right attitude towards life and so see what must be done.

It can be asked, "How can the truth of the spirit be experienced simply and practically so that the meaning can appear, so enabling one to do what is needed in life?" Perhaps this happens when men truly know that hidden in every human being is the Son of God made flesh, that "Christ in you-the hope of glory". As yet it is only a hope, but as the wheels of life carry us on from one lesson to another, we approach ever nearer to that indwelling reality where in due time is born the spirit of Christ-like qualities. Here is the true message of Christmas: that the spirit of Christ is, and must be born as a living reality into the hearts and minds of every human being.

8. HINDRANCES TO SPIRITUAL GROWTH

Spiritual study is of profound importance and one must devote to it all of oneself in time and attention, as it really involves the steady working out of truths learned into daily life. So often spiritual study is intellectually but not practically followed. Some glimmer of light may be appreciated but the working out of the laws involved makes slow progress.

Where do the hindrances lie? One main hindrance lies in the comparative newness of the western approach. The spiritual understanding flourishes in a prepared atmosphere, a magnetised environment, and in settled conditions. These conditions are difficult to find in the West where constant and frequent shifting in actions cause wide areas of disturbance.

Another hindrance may be found in the strong development of the concrete mind. Though in no way a complete detriment, yet by the intensity of its activity it hinders the down flow of inspiration from on high as a dark curtain that shuts out the light of illumination. When the concrete mind is rampant then one cannot co-operate with the higher lives on the inner side of life. That is, not unless love intervenes. For the mind separates by its analytical nature, while love attracts; the mind builds barriers by its very thinking, while love breaks down barriers and fuses together. The mind repels by a powerful vibration, while love gathers all to itself. Finally, the mind destroys, while love heals.

A third hindrance exists in the emphasis that has been laid on the material side of things. This has resulted in the world of the spirit not being recognised in a scientific sense. It may be recognised innately by spiritualists and all true sensitives, but science does not recognise it and this has an inhibiting effect upon the mass of people. For what with science saying that there is no God or spirit within man, and organised religion saying that there must be a God, the people are confused. They do not want a God constructed out of the brains of theologians. We find,therefore that the true inner comprehension finds no room for expansion and thus, those activities which should be finding their expression in a higher aspiration do turn upon themselves to the glorification of things physical - hence the emphasis on the material side of things.

Out of this grows another condition that hinders the progress of man; and that is, that a right apprehension of the future of mankind does not exist. When the physical life is concentrated upon to the exclusion of the spirit, then the true goal of existence disappears and the proper incentive to right living is lost. Then the words "let us eat and drink for tomorrow we die" characterises the attitude of the majority. Thus man deadens the inner voice that bears witness to the life hereafter and drowns the words that echo in the silence by the noise and whirl of business, pleasure and the search for excitement.

The whole secret of treading the spiritual life depends on the attitude of mind that one brings to life. When that attitude is one of concrete materialism and a desire only for the things of the moment, then little progress can be made into apprehending the higher life. Certain paramount realisations must precede the work of removing these hindrances and they might be described as:- 1) a realisation that by close attention to one's daily duties and the highest known form of truth lies the path of further revelation, for it is in the experiences of life that our attitudes are developed. 2) A realisation that in a blending of the extremes and a finding of the middle way that leads to the heart of true living.

As a man seeks to control his thinking mind so a parallel activity of the soul takes place, increasing in its own power. Love is the basic expression of the soul. Intelligent activity and loving wisdom must be brought into a balanced unity and that unity must take place in the physical in order that man might act as distributors and interpreters of divine energy. This is the "Life more abundant" that the Christ spoke about. This is the objective of our work: to turn human beings into spiritual entities through the gains of experience in the human family.

9. SPIRITUAL VALUES

Unfoldment and experience should ever be linked together, for each produces the other. As one is subjected to experience of any nature, a paralleling unfoldment brings about a constant changing of ideas with a consequent shifting in one's attitude of mind towards deeper spiritual values, so leading into newer experiences. Experiences of an ever-wider nature where-by one gains a finer appreciation of those spirit laws that govern all life. Hence we can understand the frequent reaction of those that seek a spiritual understanding to life, in that there is no point of peace to be found simply because you can never be static in life. One is constantly changing adjusting to new conditions, both physical and spiritual, and learning to live at that point of balance between the two where it is realised that the two are in fact one life unfolding through experience.

So mankind passes through stages of awareness in the unity of all life. First, he thinks that the physical form is all that there is, and the physical life engrosses his entire attention. Now this is one sense of unity, and sooner or later is lost in an awareness that there is another part of man. Then he talks of a higher and lower 'man self,' a spiritual man and a physical man. This stage begins with the learning that man is a spirit entity temporarily confined in a physical body. Of course for a long time his thinking remains predominately physical, until gradually this changes and very slowly there comes a kind of balancing where neither the physical nor the spiritual holds sway. This is when a state of apparent inertia prevails and where little appears to be accomplished in either direction. This is a negative balance. A balance that will only change into a positive one when a man's whole being becomes absorbed into the consciousness of spirit values, with the emphasis being on values and not whether one is in the physical world or the spirit world, for then it is realised that the physical is indeed spirit on a lower vibration and therefore all is unity.

So it might be asked, "what principles can guide a man towards a correctly balanced outlook in a world of spiritual values?" Study and prayerful meditations are factors that seek to draw the physical and spiritual together, and the law learning is through living experience. Seek out those aspects of truth that embody a little of the ideas on which God bases all He does; and the basis of all God's actions is love in activity. The fundamental idea which connects God and man is the power of love to drive onward. Call it evolution if you like, but it is this love that causes all motion and the urging of all men to unfold what lies within them. Hence love should be the basis of all activity, for all activity that is founded on love must lead to a divine expression of a fuller life, perfectly balanced and more adequately complete.

There is the love that governs the life of the lower self, dealing with the activities of the physical and embodied in those commonly accepted rules of decent living of which the Ten Commandments are a fine example, all having to do with the building of character. This love is learnt through the life of man as he tries to grasp and hold on to what he considers to be good and beautiful. Then by subsequent painful experiences he learns that this is only temporal and cannot be held, but only handled and passed through, as a stepping stone into the higher love that governs the higher self, dealing with those actions that demonstrate as wisdom. This love is learnt through service to others and is the highest good.

When man learns to look away from the things of his personal self, and through service to others comes to know the true power of love; when asking nothing for himself, and transcending the actions of his lower self he substitutes love and wisdom, then he can begin to understand the scope of that greater life of which all are a part and towards which mankind unfolds through the pathway of living experience. God through Christ.

10.   TRUE VALUES

Man throughout his life's experiences is presented with innumerable choices, which gradually shift from the realm of the tangible into that of the intangible. As he attracts, or is attracted, by the life of his environment, he becomes increasingly conscious of a series of shifting values until there comes that point where the pull or attraction of the spirit behind all things is more potent than the factors which have attracted him before. Then it is that his sense of values is no longer determined by the satisfaction of his material wants, nor by the desires of his emotions, nor by the pull and pleasures of the mind and intellect. He becomes strongly attracted by his soul, and this produces a tremendous revolution to his entire life, regarding the word "revolution" in its true sense, as a complete turning around. This revolution is happening now on such a large scale that it is one of the main factors producing the present explosion of experimental ideas. This experiment leads to experience, and experience leads to a wiser use of the inner powers processed by all men and to a growing appreciation of a truer world of values and realities. All this is attained by an effort on men's part to identify themselves with the world of spiritual values, and not of material values. So the world of spiritual values becomes gradually the world of true happiness, and the selection of one's interests. The use to which one puts in time and energy are all conditioned by these spiritual values.

One of the most difficult things today is to prove to men that the old and recognised values of the physical world must be relegated to their rightful place in the background of man's consciousness, and that the spirit realities behind all that is, must be for him in the immediate future, the main centre of attraction. When men grasp this, and live by its knowledge, then much of that which now holds and misleads the world must slowly disappear.

If you ponder on this, you will recognise how the great crisis of the World War did much useful work in destroying the glamorous material security in which men were living, and so destroyed much of their selfishness. Today the group is being recognised as of major importance, and the welfare of the individual is important just as far as he is an integral part of the whole.

This will not destroy initiative or individuality. It is only in the early experiments and through the inexpertness of men that you are seeing some sad mistakes. The sense of insecurity which is such a distressing aspect of the present, is simply due to this destruction of the old sense of values, bringing with it an attendant fear. This has to be broken up, for it bars the way to the values of a new age and a new world. The great thought form which man's greed and materiality have built down the ages is being steadily demolished, and mankind is on the verge of a liberation which will take him on to the path of returning to the Godhead. A liberation which comes from a free choice wisely used and applied to the good of the whole, and always conditioned by love. Note that I used the word "Wisely". Wisdom motivated by love and intelligence applied to world problems is much needed today, and sadly is not yet to be found.

Let us then learn to love with wisdom, that we might see the reality emerging out of the darkness, for the darkness is now in the process of being dispelled because men everywhere are turning round in their outlook to life, the true revolution of mankind.

11. THE PLACE OF RELIGION

The thoughts of men have ever been religious. There has never been a time when the thoughts of men about God and about life have not been present. Even the most primitive of races have always recognised a power and have attempted to define their relationship to that power in terms of fear or sacrifices. From the beginnings of native worship and idol worship, mankind has built up a structure of truth, imperfect as yet, but have laid the foundations of the future temple of truth when the light of God will be seen and proved.

Out of the darkness of time have emerged the great religions. Though diverse in theologies and forms of worship, they are united in their basic aspects. They are united in their teachings as to the nature of God and man, in their symbolism, and in certain fundamental truths. When men acknowledge this and succeed in isolating that inner structure of truth which is the saint in all climes and races, then there will emerge that universal religion, unified though not uniform in their approach to God. Dogmas will not be necessary when faith is based on experience, and the power of the church over the people will be supplanted by the power of the awakened soul in men, who know themselves as the sons of the Father, with all the characteristics which are His.
-

But in the meantime what do we have? Only a breaking away from established tradition and a revolt from authority; a tendency towards the overthrowing of old barren thought in races and faiths. Hence we are passing through a stage of questioning, rebellion and apparent licence. Out of the medley of ideas, religions, and organizations, two main lines of thought are emerging. One is doomed to die out; the other to strengthen and grow until it, in its turn, gives birth to a formulation of truth, which will suffice for the next age. These two lines are:-I) Those who look back to the past and hang on to the old ways of finding truth. These are the people who demand an authority, whether of a prophet or a bible, and prefer obedience to that authority. They are distinguished by their devotion to a church or to a cause. To them is committed the task of crystallization and defining the old truths so that the minds of men will be clarified and essentials or non—essentials be recognised for what they are. Thus the fundamental ideas underlying all religions will be discovered.   2) Those people, as yet a small minority but a growing one, who are aware of the spirit behind all things who belong to no religious organization and who have isolated the essential spiritual teachings of all religions and who may use any bible or holy writ with equal freedom. They are the unifying principle, which will eventually save the world. To them is given the task of re-organising the thoughts of men in order that that the mind may be controlled, and brought into that reflective condition which will permit it to recognise the unfolding of the spirit-within and its divine qualities.

So to the problems occupying the attention of all living at this time of unrest. Though the whole situation may seem clouded, bear in mind that when disturbance is general, as now, and whole areas involved, then the end is near. In nature a general storm clears the atmosphere and ushers in a period of more grateful living conditions. So to those who with patience carry on the work of the spirit; who keep the inner calm; who lose sight of themselves, and bearing only in mind those spiritual forces that are working through all forms and seasons, will see order brought out of chaos, construction out of past destruction and present adjustments. Hold on to the inner vision and have the long patience which endures. The problem of this transition period is the necessity for the giving out of teachings which will enable the enquirer to find himself. Hence the need for the laws of the spirit to be made clear to those who seek to know themselves, for with knowledge comes growth and skill in experience.

12. RELIGION OF THE NEW AGE

The religion of the new age already exists in spirit realms seeking recognition and life. Yet at this time the need for an utterly new venture, or for a new presentation of truth do not exist.   Nature and evolution move with gentle graduation and not with any violent breaks. The masses of public opinion need a form with which they are familiar with and in the west that form takes shape in the Christian church. Therefore that form of Christianity will basically remain. But the grip of the churches on the minds of the peoples, with its old modes of thought and interpretation must be purified, enlarged, and the truth that has ever been present, hidden, and misinterpreted be released and recognised. For it is surely easier to guide the masses into a newer light of truth if that light is poured onto familiar ground. The people must be given the chance to see and hear and be offered the opportunity to weigh and judge the significance of reality.

In the process of transmuting the old form so as to release the imprisoned life, there are two things to be held in view. First the general public is dominated by the concrete mind and is unable to grasp abstractions. It is the forms which matter the most to them. Secondly, the form of the churches, like all else, is but a temporary expedient which serves as a transient resting place for an evolving life. Eventually there must appear the Church Universal when the outpouring of the Christ Principle has been accomplished.

In answer to this need of today there has been called into being a nucleus of advanced souls through which the spirit power might flow, teaching no revolutionary doctrine or clinging to any reactionary ideas, but to demonstrate in tolerance and open-mindedness the power of the basic life of the spirit that can be found in any familiar religious structure, once the old forms that restrained them have been shattered.

And now what can we all do to nurture this change from static organisation to living organisms? In a world full of unrest; full of pain; sorrow and strife, a world in which religion exists but the life has gone; where science is prostituted to the ends of money and hate. We inhabit a world in which faith is often the subject of scoffing and where unselfishness is regarded as the attribute of a fool. Is this the atmosphere in which the spirit of Christ can breathe? Is this the atmosphere in which the spirit of God can work and live? Are the vibrations of our planet in harmony and capable of responding to the spirit of the great lives in spirit, who try to guide the pathways of mankind? We know that it is not so. What then can we do?

First, teach the laws of the spirit of man, and his sure growth towards perfection.

Secondly, live harmoniously and in love, for the violent vibrations of our surroundings must be stilled by a strong counter-vibration of love. Remembering ever that the power of the Godhead itself is with us. Naught can withstand the steady pressure of love and harmony when applied long enough. It is a long sustained pressure, which eventually breaks down the walls of division.

Thirdly, stand for all that tends to bring people towards an understanding of the basic unity in all life, for the objective is helping the powers of spirit in pouring of their goodness over the earth, and it's for us to provide a centre of peace, power and love as a spiritual uplift for all the world.

Work must be done in healing to demonstrate that the power to heal still lies in the hands of the followers of Christ. Man has to look far deeper to the causes of so many of his diseases. He must learn that he is far more than just the physical body.

Every preparation must be made to the developing of the higher psychic powers, for it is when the difference between etheric and astral forms, between true spirit clairvoyance and the clairvoyance of the lower counterparts, is understood with the laws that control the subtle bodies through which the spirit of man expresses itself. Then will more intelligent and useful work be offered towards the construction of the Church Universal.

Then the confining forms of a church, society, fraternity, or group will have served its purpose. Its structure shall crystallise and become vulnerable, so will easily be destroyed. A new form shall take its place. Watch and see if this is not so. In the infancy of mankind the forms endured for a very long time, and evolution moved very slowly. But now as the spirit of man is rising within him the form has but short duration. It lives vitally for a brief period; with rapidity it moves through its cycle and disintegrates to be succeeded by another. This rapidity must increase and not decrease as the inner expanding life of mankind vibrates to a more rapid rate of rhythm.

Therefore, you who know of these times and can interpret them aright in the light of the spirit, must ever draw closer together for the rending of service, and to help the brotherhood of master souls of which Christ is tne divine leader, in creating and maintaining the impulse towards the Church Universal as a living structure on the physical earth.

13. THE KINGDOM OF GOD ON EARTH

It is important to realise that something new is happening on earth today. It is no exaggeration to say that what is being born within the hearts of men is indeed the Kingdom of God on earth. 'Being born,' because mankind as a whole has undertaken a great shift in consciousness, and has thus arrived at a love of his fellow men, for in spite of all appearances the hearts of men are good and sound.

How can we play an effective part in this shift of focus? Surely by following the pattern laid down by the Christ, and in losing our self-interest for the interests and good of those groups of lives in which we live, work, and play. We must carry forward as a group the love and understanding for others. Hence we must, first and foremost, constantly remember that we are learning to work as a group, and that we are not trying to perfect ourselves separately from those around us. We have to learn to supplement and complement each other in the sum of our better qualities and to blend and unify, so that each can work in close rapport and spiritual cooperation with each other. This inevitably takes time, and the success of this effort will depend upon a non-critical attitude and the pouring forth of the spirit of love. This is not easy because so many good people today have an over-development of the analytical mind.

Each one of us has to learn to subordinate our own ideas of personal spiritual growth to the growth of the group requirements, in order that a spirit of service may be fostered and expanded. For the human spirit grows as it serves others, and never does it feed on the ambitions of self-centred advancement. So it may be that some people will have to slow down their spirit's progress in certain directions while others will have to hasten it. This will happen automatically if the group spirit is the dominant factor in the thoughts of each, while all desire for spiritual growth and for spiritual satisfaction is relegated to a secondary place.

Watch with care all thoughts anent each other and all suspicions and criticism must be killed. Seek instead to hold each other unwaveringly in the light of love, for you have no idea of the potency of such an effect , or of its power to release each other's bonds. By the power of love we can draw each other to those masters and teachers on the inner side of life, and so arrive a little closer to the gateway of useful service. We have this opportunity to demonstrate to each other the scientific value of love, regarded as a force in nature. Love is not a sentiment or an emotion; nor is it any desire to do the right thing in daily life. It is a wielding of the forces which guide the worlds and which is God himself in action. This love is a hard thing to cultivate, such is the inherent selfishness of human nature, and its expression demands of us the utmost that we have to give.

Can we give this? Can we aid the work of drawing forth the light of the souls in men to serve each other? The need is for channels that will work under direction in order that the knowledge of the spirit may be transmuted into wisdom, and that all our undertakings may be in harmony with the plans of God for all mankind.

14.   THE PATH

There has long been a tendency to wrap up the matter of treading the Path in mystery and to think of it as setting apart, as special, those who undertake the effort. In fact it does no such thing, for all men are treading the Path in their own way, time, and circumstances, because all are sparks of the divine. The only difference is that some people recognise their divine destiny sooner than others, and so are able to take up the always present opportunity of starting to walk more directly towards mankind's common goal.

In taking up this opportunity men take into their own hands the responsibility for accomplishing their destiny; and no man is truly treading the Path who is not helping others to find and tread it also. This meeting of others' needs is a vital part of treading the Path. It need not be glamorous or dramatic, for it is not given to all men to serve grandly, but it is given to all men to serve to their highest achievable capacity, knowing that as need is met, the capacity to meet greater needs unfolds . Ever remember that Jesus served at home for a number of years, undergoing that most difficult experience of home life with its unvaried routine and its lessons of service and understanding of human need. This is the point that every spiritual pilgrim has to start from. Until divinity is expressed in the home amongst those who know you well, it cannot be expected to express itself elsewhere. "The place where you are now is the place from which your spiritual journey begins, and not the place from which you escape". It is here in the place you now are, that the real spirit tests begin. A test is something which tries your strength, and daily life does this with searching thoroughness. It is easy to imagine that you would make a success of treading the Path and living a spiritual life if only you had different opportunities, or somebody else's capacity or circumstances. In actual fact each person has exactly the environment, and set of circumstances, best designed to call into activity the spirit hidden deep within his own being. Everyone has those contacts in the world which he or she needs to be able to take the next step. It is by taking this next step that men learn to tread with confidence the path of the spirit that leads from the unreal to the real.

With life firmly rooted in simplicities such as these, it becomes possible to achieve definite spirit recognitions. Those next necessary steps, so easily measured in your daily lives, can lead to goals so high that the human mind cannot comprehend them. Nonetheless, give thought to these high objectives for towards them the Path inevitably leads. Every effort to comprehend and visualise them, however faintly, sends forth tenuous threads of understanding, which in time will develop into bridges by means of which man is enabled to pass into higher experiences.

This makes it clear that the really major step to be taken is a shift of consciousness and an attitude of mind - a stepping up of the vibratory quality of the total life. It is not given to serious students of the spirit to stand still. A recognition achieved and an experience undergone - these are the points from which the next expansion of spirit consciousness must begin. In the light of these possibilities which lie open to you, treading the Path becomes an enterprise so splendid, so creative, so demanding, that nothing less than total involvement in it is possible. You are offered the opportunity, made aware of the needs and assured of the results. To make the decision and the actual taking of the required steps are matters of individual concern. The Path is there: it is not easily found, though approaches leading to it are many and various. It is not trodden easily, despite the many signposts available. Yet it can be found and it can be trodden by those with a purposeful persistence.

15. LOVE YOUR NEIGHBOUR AS YOURSELF

"Love your neighbour as yourself" This call by the Christ has as yet been given very little proper attention. We have loved ourselves, and sought to love those we like. But to love universally and because our neighbours are of the same spirit make up as ourselves with a nature latently perfect and whose destiny is infinite, have always been regarded as a beautiful dream to be brought about in a future so distant, and in a heaven so far away , that we may well forget all about it.

Two thousand years have nearly passed since the greatest expression of God's love walked on earth and bade us love each other. Yet we still fight and hate, using our powers for selfish ends and directing our living for personal gain. Have we considered what the world would have been like today if men had listened to the Christ and sought to obey His command? Surely mankind should have made war impossible and should have reduced crime to the minimum, for what is crime but selfishness run wild. Surely we should have eliminated disease because men would be living examples of divinity, in harmony with the laws of spirit and nature? But this is not the case, and hence the modern world conditions prevail.

But the spirit law must, and will be, enunciated. This can be summed up in the words :"Let a man so live that his life is harmless". Then no evil can grow out of his thoughts, his actions or his words. This is not negative harmlessness, but a difficult and positive activity. Harmlessness is the expression of the life of him who knows himself to be a spirit, and whose essential nature is love .This realization shows itself in a true comprehension of a brother's need, and seeing the inner spirit causes that are conditioning the outer life ,divorced from any sentiment or expediency. Thus is produced a correct response to true need. Harmlessness brings caution in judgement, reticence in speech, an ability to refrain from impulsive action and the cultivation of a non-critical spirit.

If this practical paraphrase of the words of Christ were universally declared and applied, we should have order growing out of chaos, and love superseding personal selfishness. This sounds like a platitude, but platitudes are recognised truths, and is not a truth a scientific pronouncement? The moulding of life's ways by the recognition of the law of Love is probably too simple to evoke an interest. But the power lying behind it is the power of divinity itself ,and the recognition is simply a matter of time. Evolution will force it at some distant date.

The forming of an earlier recognition lies in the hands of those disciples and thinkers of the present. We live at a time when one religious age is passing into another, and when the hearts of the people are becoming open to impression. Much that can be seen today of unbelief and criticism is based on the fact that religion has been superseded by creeds and dogma which have taken the place of living experience . It is this living experience that must be brought to the people. "Of what real use" you might ask. It should be pointed out that by thinking on these things, by living before one's fellow men the teachings that have been absorbed, and by living the life in conformity with the laws of the spirit, men render a service that is very real ... and service is love in action.

16. ACTION IN THE FACE OF INERTIA

We live in a time of extremes, of extreme riches and poverty, extreme ignorance and learning, extreme selfishness and self-sacrifice. On every hand can be seen the wrecking of the institutions of the past, with consequent chaos, disasters, despair and suffering. Between these extremes the mass of people sway inert, helpless and easily influenced. They have a basic good will and true intentions but are ridden by fear or a feeling of futility, and a realisation that what has to be done is so stupendous, that their little efforts are next to useless in breaking down those barriers of hate and separation that are to be found.

Out of this condition how can order be restored and the differences healed? How can the many religious groups pursue their work of leading men and women to an expression of their divinity? That is to say, to lead the people to express the spirit within each one of them: and here surely lies a clue towards that answer: in the spirit, in so far as men and women everywhere will learn of this inner source of power which binds them all together, and in its completeness is capable of moulding their ideas into the needed changes of thought. For what is going on today is the working out of ideas that lie within. The power behind these ideas lies in the world of spirit, and the people have no idea of the vast numbers of those in the spirit who join with them in their thinking. When this is realised, and everybody can steadily and quietly, with no sense of hurry, learn about and put the emphasis of their lives on the spirit of all things, then they will be reaching into the source of reality and power, from whence the true values of living can be found.

Now when knowledge is given, it must be used. It must find practical expression in daily living. Therefore, upon all of us rests a duty to mould our daily lives upon the basis of imparted truth, if it is indeed a truth. Perhaps some of us are simply interested, and treat this as a fascinating sideline to study. Perhaps it pleases some because it is a little different from the general run of given teachings. Perhaps it gives pleasure to some who think they are receiving something ahead of humanity as a whole. All these reactions are of small importance. What is important is that we attempt in no matter how small a way, to apply the truth as we see it in our lives.   Then we can help construct the thought atmosphere of the New Age teachings. We do this by the practical application of any truth that we have understood, and by the example of our lives to our fellow men.

17.   SPIRIT RESPONSIBILITIES

Today with the sweeping away of old outworn ideas and beliefs that have been the foundations of men's ideas on God, and the regulation of his social life and conduct, people everywhere are clutching at any straw that offers them a new vision or ideal. Mankind, we are assured, is on the way to a newer and richer life, but that day can only be advanced according to how the spiritually inclined people get out into the world and take up their responsibilities. That fuller life will be preceded by times of great difficulty already obvious in human affairs generally. Hence the need for the steadying and quietening effect of those people who can understand and rightly handle the new conditions that are ever arising.

Everyone who is honestly and sincerely trying to lead the true life of the spirit is going through the mill. The going is rough and consequently there is a natural tendency towards a preoccupation with personal difficulties and viewpoints, to the extent that wider responsibilities and opportunities are obscured.

You will not free yourselves from these hindrances and difficulties until you take your eyes off yourselves, and instead attune yourselves to the whole of life. This process of attuning oneself to the whole of life is usually reversed by so many into an attempt to relate the whole of life to themselves. 'Attunement' is not just a matter of intellectual comprehension or compliance; it involves a completely new adjustment of your whole being. A new state of identification is required based on the knowledge of the power of the spirit within, which is brought about by an inner growing, and an inner experiencing that can be maintained, no matter what the outer disturbances are of daily living.

At whatever stage an individual may be, he has a spiritual job to do in the physical world. It is no part of the work of the spirit to issue job-cards to anyone. This is unnecessary, for every person already has one issued to him at birth by his own soul. The ability to read what is written there depends upon the extent to which the eye of spiritual perception is open. To achieve this requires some focus on the spirit side of life, and a deep love for all mankind, based on the recognition of the unity of spirit and not on any emotional reaction.

If we are determined to help build the kingdom of God on earth, and to lift some of humanity's load, we must learn to distinguish those outer events which express God's plan from those which do not. What, you may ask, is the criterion whereby you may know which of several lines of activity is the right line to take. The choice is, and must ever be, your own and not that of others, otherwise you become as sheep, regimented in thought and action, which would be contrary to the basic law of the spirit: that of freewill. The right action to be taken must be based on the power of spirit discernment. If you haven't any, then there is only one way to learn - through experience. You must learn to discern between right and wrong, between selfish and unselfish action, between individual benefit and group responsibility; between that which separates man from man or nation from nation, and that which serves to unite. If you are lost in the interests of others, untrammelled by selfish desires, then your just obligations will be met, your responsibilities shouldered, and your work carried forward. The way will unfold and those duties that you came into the world for, will emerge.

(See also "Responsibility" 49)

18.   CONFLICT: STRESS and STRAIN

Since the dawn of history it has seemed that mankind has ever chosen to develop, grow, and evolve by way of "Conflict". To try and understand the principle behind this is very difficult to see, as it is trying to understand what is behind and responsible for all the stresses and strains in life that we all experience, and this appears to be going back to the most basic conflict of all; that conflict between the things of the physical and the things of the spirit.

Each one of us can bring our own interpretation of the working out of this basic principle, as we watch the effects in our lives of those actions brought about by stress and strain. But in the end we are brought, through tension, to realise that all this stress and strain always seems to bring us to a point of having to make a choice, in thought, action, or feeling. So we can say that conflict develops in us the power to discern what is good or not so good, and then having discerned it, brings us closer to a point of decision; not just in deciding what is good or bad, right or wrong, but it is deeper than that; in deciding whether we will conduct our lives in a spiritual manner or not. That would in fact be saying whether we accept that life has a purpose or not, and having accepted this, we would then wish to bring our individual lives into line and harmony with this purpose, for surely we would agree that this purpose is good. So now we see that this principle of conflict opens up for us many experiences wherein we can try out what we believe to be the correct things to do, in order to bring our lives into harmony with this purpose of good. All the time we will be choosing between the values of the earth and the values of spirit, ever remembering that we have the freedom of choice through that precious gift of freewill.

Slowly, very slowly, the balance of our lives swings over to the side of the spirit behind all things, as, through the many experiences, the true issues of what life is all about begin to become increasingly clear in our minds and attitudes. So we learn that the principle of conflict is a spiritual necessity to be used as an instrument to bring about the emergence of what controls us in our present stage of evolution: those unhealthy and unwholesome thoughts, emotions and deeds. It is in conflict that we learn to reject these things, as they prevent us from understanding and living as spiritual beings. It is as a result of conflict that the complete harmonising of our physical selves and the spirit nature will be brought about, and it is for this purpose that we are in this school on Earth.

What then must we do while living in this sea of tension and conflict that is our Earth at this moment? Surely it is to develop an ability to think sanely, with a balanced and correct outlook towards the spirit behind all things, while maintaining a broad and open point of view. We must always persevere in a calm and dispassionate frame of mind as we try to understand in a spirit of Love, and show in a small scale those qualities that, as far as we are able to know, must some day characterise all mankind. Don't be discouraged, but hold firmly to the conviction of the inevitable destiny of the spirituality of mankind. A perfect outcome of conflict will necessarily be lacking, for perfection is not yet possible. Nevertheless, a situation can be brought about which will permit the human spirit to rise above the material values into the clear light of spiritual perception, and there we will know the Christ, and the whole meaning of His life and teachings.

19. PAIN AND SUFFERING

Pain and suffering are for most people a mystery without reason. On every side it is apparent that men and women are bewildered by the pressures they are bearing, in many cases to their fullest capacity. In the streets of any big city stress can be seen and sensed as one of the main components of human life. As emotional and mental conflicts are taking their toll in human misery, it is becoming increasingly clear that some higher impulses and impressions are combining to impinge upon the human organism, thereby creating sharper degrees of response. This is making men and women more sensitive, thus increasing their capacity to feel and tune in to pain not only from the tangible world of the senses but also from the subtle world of the spirit.

This state of vulnerability can be viewed as a glorious prelude to entering more fully into the life of the spirit. For when the heart unfolds to encompass greater areas of suffering, then indeed man no longer lives unto himself alone, but shares a fraction of the overall weight carried by humanity and life on this planet.   Because evolution is leading us more intensely into the experience of suffering, there is a need to try and understand more about it, for only in a comprehension of underlying causes can we begin to cooperate with the purpose which is seeking to be brought about, both in individual life and in the greater life of the human race.

The capacity to suffer is directly related to the power to think, and to consciously relate cause and effect. Increased capacity to think therefore brings increased capacity to respond to pain. In the wake of this response to pain follows a resistance, being the automatic reaction to all pain impulses. This immediately sets up a field of friction within, which the human self is caught up with and all its dire results. This is to say that it is rebellion that produces pain and sorrow, a rebellion against some basic cause which must have some purpose and meaning.

To counter this response/resistance process, which enlarges the pain area to involve the whole man, we have to re-orientate our attitude of mind to one of an acceptance, being a great spiritual force or law capable of working like magic entirely beyond its apparent scope. For in effect it is an act of aligning the little will of man with the greater will of divine reason. Once suffering is accepted, its hard core seems to become absorbed in an alchemical process of transmutation and which if resisted, could become a destroying force, yet is transformed into a power for good. Then the purpose of the particular incident of suffering would be completed. The purifying ingredients having done their work, freedom is won from that particular test and also freedom from the fear of it.

As the incoming energies of the new age meet the resistance inherent in the concepts and ideas deeply rooted in the consciousness of the passing age, collective suffering of mankind will undoubtedly increase. In all fields we find organised group resistance involving human beings in friction to an almost unbelievable degree. One of the most serious aspects of the world situation today is the destroying force unleashed through the friction points in the many groups, national, international, or local which control life on this planet. The need is for a balancing, bridging capacity by men and women of goodwill, aligning their wills to God's greater will. They must be spiritually capable of connecting true causes and effects and living and exemplifying the beauty of their inner lives in their outward actions. These servants of the Christ can counter the forces of materialism, even though they may have little knowledge of the details of God's divine plans, for they intuitively follow that part of the pattern which they are destined to work out with the innate wisdom born of soul power.

All types and grades of people are needed in the great march from darkness into light which is now going on. Those whose task it is to break up outmoded forms, as well as the creative builders, the artist as well as the scientist, the contemplative as well as the workers in the field - all are needed to bring about that balance of forces, which must pertain before the presence of the Christ can be seen and felt as a reality of life on earth.

All this holds little hope of immediate alleviation for the masses, bound as they are to the wheels of suffering. As each human soul gains mastery over pain in his life and dispels the glamour of fear surrounding it, so he indirectly and infinitesimally lifts a share of his brother's burden also. As each one of us gains a more direct understanding of this human problem, we are able to enter more fully into the individual sufferings of those around us, becoming more effective and useful because we know about it and above all, because we CARE.

20.   KARMA

Karma does not   punish transgression merely for the sake of punishment even while outwardly that assumption often appears to have validity. Karma is the law that balances and harmonises under the universal adjustment mechanism relating to all causes and their effects. Without it the universe would fall into utter chaos instead of being so clearly a well-organised and regulated enterprise.

Believing therefore, that all life moves under the law of just deserts and aims to balance and co-operate in all things, that we might evaluate the evolutionary motions which seem to threaten us, what is their purpose? Surely not to inflict undeserved suffering and privation. We receive what we have earned: not only the good and the bad, but also that which provides us with the best opportunity for spiritual progress. This happens despite the surface appearances which may seem to belie this truth when a situation is viewed from a too shallow and too short a range. We need to trust the spirit to have arranged its life pattern for the best possible interests of the larger divine self which encompasses that fragment of itself: the human body.

If Karma can be viewed primarily as a benevolent teacher instead of as a punitive agent moving with fatal precision to an inevitable conclusion of its course, then much confusion and suffering could be eliminated. Therefore it is up to mankind to discover just what lessons are implied in any situation or pattern, and then to set in motion those spiritual forces which can soften the karmic effect which otherwise would run its full and possibly painful course. For instead of waiting for karma to strike head on, man can, as a creative being, by using the same energy which moves the karmic stream, mould its course considerably. He can bring about his own well-being instead of allowing nature to do it slowly by repeated stabs, stings, and pains, whenever he veers off onto unwholesome tangents. But to wield these energies he must bring his intelligence and scientific understanding, a purity of motive and sincere goodwill towards all others that will be involved. Man must learn to accept the interdependence of all forms of life on this planet. By accepting this, his present concentration on serving the self will logically give way to serving the whole, which will then reflect in the self in a way that makes for true spiritual growth.

To change undesirable effects into good, the systems and beliefs producing them must obviously be re-orientated, for man-made systems express selfish motives, but mankind as a whole can only react from that level of his awakening spirit. Men are still infants, struggling with the inner selves which they do not as yet accept as being infinitely superior to their proud outer selves. The higher spiritual faculties are potentially within man awaiting recognition as a high destiny of divinely motivated creativity.

But a God is not made: He is self-made. No one, not even God can do his growing for him. God guides and points, and man responds. He has unquestionable freedom to heed or not to heed, and certainly takes his time about it. Yet only by the working together of God and Man can anything of real value be attained. Man's mistake at this time is his attempt to go it alone, due chiefly to his pride in scientific and mechanistic achievement. This is understandable as a basis for easier and happier living conditions, which is certainly desirable and a necessary part of evolution. Yet it is not meant to be the goal in life. The primary need is spiritual growth. Materialism is an aid, not an end. True ends are still far off. They must be earned on higher levels of life. Man needs divine inspiration to live by, yet has largely substituted matter for spirit as a beacon to guide him. Materialism has to be placed in the right perspective. It has to be brought down from its present position of dominance over the lives of men to its proper place in life's pattern. The block to an effective spiritual expansion, to universal peace and a better civilization found on the culture of the spirit is that mankind is not yet adequately convinced that the road of materialism is not the true road to salvation. That road has brought him a long way, but an important turn to the brighter road illuminated by the light of the soul can get him started on the next great lap of the evolutionary spiral, where an awakened sensitivity to spiritual impression could reveal the inner powers possessed by men, and hasten the growing up when mankind can surrender to the soul's superior management of the tempo and rate of growth: his priceless heritage which raised him above the lower kingdoms ages ago.

21. SERVICE

Service is usually interpreted as exceedingly desirable though it is seldom realised how very difficult service essentially is. It involves so much sacrifice of time and interest of one's own ideas. It requires exceedingly hard work because it necessitates so much effort ,wisdom, and the ability to work without attachment. All such qualities are not easy to attain.

Service is frequently regarded as an attempt to bring people around to the point of view of the one who serves, because that one has found something good and true and useful, and believes it must necessarily be good and true and useful for all. Again, service is viewed as something we render to the poor, the afflicted, the diseased and the unhappy. Very often service can grow out of a desire to tread in the footsteps of the Christ, He who went about doing good as it is said, and setting an example that we should follow. People, therefore, do service from a sense of obedience. Service can likewise be rendered from a deep seated desire for spiritual perfection, it being regarded as one of the necessary qualifications for the spiritual life, namely that one must render some kind of service.

This is all right, true and meritorious, but the motives behind it are all entirely wrong. Yet in spite of all the wrong motives, service of a kind is constantly and readily being rendered in welfare movements, in philanthropic endeavours, in Red Cross work, in educational uplifts and in the task of relieving distressing world conditions. How then do we define "Service"? Service can briefly be defined as the spontaneous effect of soul contact. It is the manner whereby the nature of the soul can demonstrate itself in the world of human affairs. Service is not a quality or a performance. It is not an activity towards which people must strive. It is a soul urge, and as such, is as much as the urge of self-preservation and is a demonstration of the physical nature of man. It is a soul instinct, and the outstanding characteristic of the soul.

Service, therefore, cannot be taught or imposed upon a person. It is simply the first real evidence upon the physical world of the fact that the soul is beginning to express itself. Neither theory nor aspiration will or can make a man a real server. How then is it that there is so much activity in service demonstrated in the world today? Simply because the life ,words, and deeds of the Christ have had an effect, and so men earnestly attempt to imitate his example, little realising that imitation does not net true results, but only indicates a growing possibility. This possibility first demonstrates as the life of the spirit working in a man's own nature, for the first thing the soul has to do is to make a man aware that he is a living principle of divinity, and then to prepare his lower nature so that it will offer no impediment to the life which must and will pour through it. This is the first and hardest task. When the natural impetus of the man in incarnation is to be the expression of his soul, then the life pouring through him, gently and naturally, will have an effect upon his environment and his associates. This effect can then be called a "life of Service", which shows itself in real understanding and true helpfulness. As the flow of spiritual life becomes stronger, so will the life effect spread. It will not be planned, nor will it be fought for as an end in itself. It will be a natural expression with the soul taking form and direction according to a man's past experience, and conditioned by the times, race and age. It will be a living flow of spontaneous effusion of power and love from soul levels.

22.   SEEK AND YE SHALL FIND:- Seek out the ways

As students of the spirit life we may well look upon ourselves as exploring our shared experiences and meditations, and feeling some satisfaction in the knowledge that we are finding some answers to what we seek.   Let us consider now what it is that we wish to find ? Is it a dim perspective of great heights to be scaled in what we imagine as spiritual advancement, or is it as our brother of the East would say "seek out the way" - that pathway in life that is sought for its own sake without regard to what benefits we may receive. It is not very flattering to find that so much of our longing to study and to render service has a basically selfish origin, resting on a desire for liberation or distaste for the humdrum duties of everyday.

The true seeker of the way of life is he who avails himself to receive with an open mind and with an inner longing and who recognises that there is something more than all the physical knowledge and accumulated experience.   Nothing will satisfy him until he finds that centre of his being where he is at home with his God and Father.   This calls for hard work, intelligent unfoldment, steady aspiration, and the inner perception which sees the world as it really is.   It calls for the capacity to submerge and lose sight of the personal lower nature in the task of seeking guidance under soul impulse. Above all it calls for courage: courage to run counter to the world's opinion, and to the very best of scientific opinion at that.   For having learned to see things as they really are in their spirit essence you have to learn to do the right things as you know them, irrespective of the opinions of the earth's greatest and most quoted.   It is here that most seekers fail.   They do not do the very best that they know about in their hearts.   They fail to act as their inner voice tells them.   They leave undone those things which they are prompted to do in their moments of reflection and inner quiet, and fail to speak the word which the spirit urges them to speak.

The best exponent of the spiritual life is he who lives each day in the place where he is, and does not live in the place where he thinks he should be. Too often men fail to make good where they are because they find some reason which makes them think they should be elsewhere. Men run away, almost without realising it, from difficulties and inharmonious conditions, from places which involve problems, and from circumstances which call for action of a higher sort, and which has been staged to draw out the best that is in them.   Thus men flee from themselves instead of seeking out the life, and to seek out the life is to live the life, and to live the life is to live as an example for others, for what after all is "service" but the living of a life of example that other seekers may find what you reveal.

23.   GOD IMMANENT

God transcendent, greater, vaster, and more inclusive than the worlds of His own creation is universally recognised, and has been generally emphasised. God transcendent has dominated the religious thinking of millions of spiritually minded people down through the centuries, which have passed since mankind has begun to press forward towards the Godhead.

Slowly there is dawning upon the awakening minds of men the great paralleling truth of God Immanent: God within, divinely pervading all known forms, conditioning from within all the kingdoms in nature, and expressing innate divinity through human beings. The nature of that divine immanence was portrayed two thousand years ago in the person of the Christ. Today, as a result of this unfolding divine presence, there is entering into the minds of men everywhere the concept of "Christ in us: The hope of Glory" as Saint Paul expressed it. There is a growing and developing belief that Christ is in us as He was in the Master Jesus, and this belief, as it becomes established, will alter mankind's entire attitude to life.

The wonder of that life, lived two thousand years ago, is still with us having lost none of its freshness. It is an eternal inspiration, hope, encouragement and an example. The love that He demonstrated then still holds the thinking world in thrall, even though relatively few have really attempted to demonstrate the same quality of love as HE did, a love that will unerringly lead one into a life given to the service of others, to a complete self-forgetfulness and into a radiant magnetic living. The words that He spoke were few and simple, being quite capable of being understood by all men and women, but their significance has been largely lost in the welter of intricate legalities of theological commentators since Christ lived and left us: or apparently left us.

For today Christ is as near to humanity as he ever was. He is closer than the most aspiring and hopeful seeker ever dreams. For Christ belongs to Humanity, to the world of men and women, and not to any one Church or faith alone.   Around Him are gathered the masters of the wisdom and all those liberated souls, sons of the Father who down the ages have passed from the darkness into the light, from the unreal into the real. They are all waiting, under Christ's guidance, to reveal to all those who struggle in the storms of world affairs that they are not alone, and that God transcendent is working to bring relief, while God immanent is on the verge of being recognised. Behind them is the great succession of those in the spirit world who are posed for activity: a succession of those who have lived on earth, who have accepted the fact of God all around and discovered the reality of God within. It is essential that today there should be a measure of this knowledge concerning these things. This should be expounded in no fanatical or prophetic spirit, nor as a speculative theologian nor as an exponent of wishful thinking; but there are many who know that the time is right, and that the appeal of faithful hearts has penetrated to the highest spiritual spheres, and there set in motion spirit forces which cannot be stopped. The cry of humanity is today at such a volume, that it has given rise to activities in the spirit world that can and must result in the transformation of the divine will into human good-will.

Now surely, religion is the name which we give to the invocative appeal of humanity which leads to the response of the spirit of God. That spirit works in every heart and in all groups. It impels the Christ to take action, and that action that He is now taking will lead to him being known and felt by all men.

24. GUIDANCE

The question of guidance is a difficult one to handle, for it is based on an instinctive recognition of God and God's plans for men. We may define guidance as that intuition whereby a man becomes aware of inclinations, voices, impressed commands or revelations of what course of conduct should be pursued, together with a general indication of what lines of activity "God" is proposing to those who are attentive. When in this state of awareness a man may permanently change his way of life, or it may have a temporary effect once the initial urge to respond has exhausted itself.

Now the blind, unreasoning, subjection of oneself to any guidance, whatever its source, would render a man a negative, impressionable automaton, and should this happen, a man would be forfeiting his most divine possession, that of free will. There is no fear of this, however, for intelligent men and women are always available to think on these things. Mankind is intended to be the intelligent arbiter of his own destiny and the conscious exponent of his own divinity, of the God within. For this reason we should watch carefully for the possible sources of what is guiding our thoughts and actions, and so learn that the whole subject is very vast and complicated, it being a part of wisdom to ascertain the origin of what is guiding us.

First, there is the direct guidance or instruction from a man or woman about the physical world to whom one may turn for help. This is largely a brain relationship, which is greatly helped by the fact that the seeker knows within himself pretty well what the instructor would say in any given circumstance. Then there is the introverted attitude that brings to the surface all the subconscious desires, which, when given a religious direction, is interpreted as the voice of God giving guidance. Then there can be the recovery of old spiritual aspirations coming from a previous life or lives. These are hidden deeply in one's nature and can be brought to the surface when given some kind of stimulation. They then appear as utterly new and so regarded as divine injunctions. They have, however, always been present in the inner nature. Guidance can also be recorded telepathically, as the result of tuning in upon the minds of others and with which one may have an affinity. Guidance is always coming from all types and kinds in the spirit world, ranging from the very good to the very bad. They include the help offered by great masters' souls through those who work for them. Ever remember that no true spirit master will seek to control any person by giving a positive command on what to do; they will always suggest, or speak in terms of a general talk. Hence the many misinterpretations of so called guidance.

Transcending all these can come the guidance from a man's own soul through meditation, prayer, discipline and service to others. This, when clear and direct, is true guidance coming as it is from the inner spark of the divine which is in every human being. When there is a true and right understanding of this inner divine voice, then and only then, can one say one has an infallible guidance, and then it is that the inner God can speak with clarity to its instrument - man upon the physical world.

christmas rose

25. PRAYER

However you may define prayer, we know that the human activity called prayer could not and would not have come into use unless there had been a spontaneous desire on man's part to address a higher practice. It is certain that in moments of crisis all down the ages men have found comfort and assurance by seeking communion with a unseen God.

There are of course many ways of praying and many different kinds of prayer. The simplest and most general method is the expression of a desire whose results can be tested: the prayer for peace in time of war, for health in sickness, and for safe deliverance from dangers. What we want or would like to happen, we pray for, hoping to expedite the matter.

 Clear thought, intense desire and absolute faith in what is prayed for must bring about its materialisation. The child who with complete confidence kneels by the bedside and requests a gift of God which he wants with his whole being and is quite sure he is going to get it, will most certainly have his prayer answered. Remembering the reception of what has been prayed for does not necessarily bring the anticipated result; as for instance, money is one of those things recognised as being powerless to bring the happiness children associate with it.

If this form of prayer is the only form we know, then small wonder that we cast it off as we grow in the spirit. Experience teaches us that our needs, desires and wishes fluctuate from day to day, and may be in opposition to the needs, desires and wishes of others who may be more important than ourselves in the scheme of things. So we learn that the longest view is usually the best view, and that a day- to- day focus does not give us a wide enough range to be able to decide what are the best things to pray for. We then modify our petitions with the rider that "These things are asked for only if they are in accordance with thy will." Thus acknowledging that with our limited knowledge, understanding and foresight, we are liable to make mistakes both on our own behalf and for others.

Directly we add this rider to our petitions, we cancel out the power of desiring, and into the childlike but blind faith, we throw doubt. " If it be thy will." We are now not sure of the rightness of our prayers. We acknowledge our inability to see things in true perspective, and we now offer that intense desire that forced into manifestation answers to our child-like prayers to God, to use for his own end. We no longer limit this power to our own little need, but ask that they be used for the greatest good from God's viewpoint. So the experience of anyone who would serve God is to change his focus of attention from what he wants to do for God, to what is the plan of God for him. Prayer then is used as a channel of communication saying, " This seems to be what is required; if I am right, help me. If I'm wrong, direct me anew."

But prayer development does not stop there. The prayer of the really mature in spirit desires nothing, not even the knowledge of serving God. " I want", was the first stage of prayer. " I want but only if it is thy will", the second. " Thy will only", must be the eventual expression. When this is the prayer of our life, then all of our mental, emotional and physical equipment will be at the service of the soul within, which never operates from personal good but for the good of all.

We reveal ourselves in Prayer: what we prayer for, and how we pray. Christ demonstrated his son-ship of God through his prayers, which were always for the benefit of those around him. He stressed the need for prayer and quiet communion with the highest, in order that the day -to -day stresses of life could be met with an abundance of life.

Thus in prayer we demonstrate our absolute confidence in a power behind the universe that is vitally concerned with our world. It is in prayer that we bear witness to our knowledge that mankind is an instrument of God's purpose. It is to call forth from the hearts, minds and the souls of our fellow men an understanding, a yearning, and a belief that they too are concerned with God, of equal value and importance in bringing to pass His will. It is to keep us sensitive to God's purpose by keeping the channel between Him and our souls open, so that minds and hearts are able to demonstrate in physical living, the ways of God.

26. SIN

The theme of sin runs naturally and normally through human history.
The belief in an angry God who exacted penalties for all that is done by mankind is as old as man himself. The idea of a God whose nature is love has battled with the idea of a God whose nature is wrath.

As mankind has developed mentally, there has been a consequent development of a conscience which has the capacity to have a sense of values, and as a result of this, the ability to see the higher and lower natures in opposition to each other. When the higher self with its values and range of contacts is instinctively felt, and the lower self with its lesser values and more material range of activities is realised, it follows that a sense of division and of failure is developed. Men realise their lack of achievement.

How then shall we look upon sin? God is love; and love is unity and at one-ment in harmony. Man being divine in nature has to love. Sin, therefore, is an infringement of the law of love as we show it in our relations with God or with our brother men — all being sons of God. It is doing those things from the purely selfish interest which brings suffering and distress to those around us: our families, our social contacts, our business associates, or just any human being with whom destiny casts us, no matter for how brief a moment. This brings us to realise that sin signifies a wrong relationship with other human beings. It is beginning to dawn upon men today that the real sin is to hurt another human being. Sin is the misuse of our relationship with each other, and there is no evading these relationships; they exist. We live in a world of men and our lives are spent in contact with each other. Our task is to express our divinity in the same way that the Christ expressed it; in harmless living and ceaseless service to our fellow men.

We all know at least one thing in our lives which is not right, some thought or action which is contrary to God's plan for us. Until and unless we straighten out that wrong, it is profitless to ask what may be the next step in God's plan for us. If, however, we are ready to conform to God's plan in this one respect in which we know it, then experience shows that the "Still small voice from within" will tell us the next thing God wishes us to do. It may be to right some other wrong; it may be a happy thought in regard to some work that could be done, it may be an untried approach in some personal relationship. It may be a flash of insight into new truth, but as long as we refuse to take the first step, it is unreasonable to expect God to show us the next. Nor, if he did, would it do us any good.

27.   FREEDOM

Freedom is a concept, which changes with circumstances. Depending upon what these have been, we have had the great movements calling for political freedom: freedom for slaves, and the economic freedoms from want and fear. Behind all these freedoms over which men have fought and died, there lies a great truth: the goal of all freedom is the freedom of the spirit. All other freedoms are simply introductions to this "The Great Freedom".

Governments spend huge sums of money in establishing freedom from want and fear among their own people, but what is the sense of trying to make men economically free whilst they remain slaves to their own thoughts and feelings? Men are the victims of their own thinking, and in order to approach any freedom of the spirit, they have to learn to watch and control their attitudes of thought. For can it not be agreed that all freedoms from any political or economic restrictions have been made possible, only in the degree to which the people have voluntary replaced a self-control for the external controls imposed before?

Everyone at a certain stage in the evolution of his personality wonders about the way to understand and explore the real purpose of his soul on earth. To question the reason of his existence and the meaning of life. When he has grown to this stage and when the urge is sufficiently strong, then he begins to study himself. In the great laboratory of his thoughts, he soon distinguishes between his higher and lower states of consciousness and so he begins to define himself in terms of basic inner attitudes and qualities. Thus do we begin to observe society in terms of motives.

At that stage we can understand the struggle of the spirit within seeking its own freedom, rising as it were to the surface at such times when our thoughts and aspirations make it possible, and at other times being overwhelmed by our lower self. This struggle of two conscious states is the reason behind all struggles for freedom. One is struggling with this conquest in all daily living, and looking around we see mountains of unnecessary obstacles occupying so much thought going into everything under the sun except the one thing that matters; the growth of the spirit within.

How shall we cultivate the garden of ourselves? By ploughing up and throwing out the accumulated weeds and rubbish which choke our outlooks of thought and feelings. Most people's outlook may be described as purely physical, selfish and personal, or as an attempt to digest other people's mistakes, so the first job is to cleanse ourselves of the poison of unconscious human thought. When the garden of ourselves is somewhat cleared, we shall find certain seeds left which are well worth planting. These are our ideals, hopes and aspirations, the seeds of spirit. After they have grown a bit, we will find our thoughts are deepening; our emotions become quieter and life more simplified. We enter into inner worlds of thoughts and feelings. It is then that we find moments when our higher selves are something completely separate from the lower self. We can clearly see the difference between our highest inspired state and those lower selfish selves. Now we understand the meaning of "to live on the earth, but not be a part of it"; to live a life through humanity and yet stand free from all that holds us to it. Is this the freedom of the spirit? To raise men beyond themselves.

When man everywhere begins to interpret events and happenings in the world as expressions on men's motives and attitudes of thought, they are taking the early steps into seeing underlying causes. Then perhaps men might ask why they think and feel as they do and so realise the struggle of the inner spirit to rise above the lower self. The lower self thinks lowly. Free your souls, and awaken to the greatness of the future. Refuse to think wrongly.

28. OLD AGE

When men and women reach that time of life referred to as "Three score years and ten" they are often, from the spiritual point of view, confronted with a choice of whether they have reached a high water mark in their development, and therefore rest on their well earned laurels, or whether there is still to be found in them springs of interest and those inner urges which will enable them to reach further in the life of a living soul.

Men and women go through many years of necessary divided effort of meeting family and social commitments, as well as the calling of work for the spirit. Then when outer obligations lessen and demands on one's time and attention diminish, they close their minds to the opportunities which are opening up, and all because of the powerful illusion of "Old Age". Surely, instead of regarding physical old age as a period of withdrawal, we should realise that the spiritual opportunities are multiplying.

The important factor in all this is one's awareness and attitude of mind to the things of the spirit. What better period for this to blossom in all its beauty than in those years when physical desires fade a little, and the pressures of duties and time are eased. These are in fact years of opportunity to expand the growth of the spirit within. This is not something that can be impaired by physical fatigue, for whatever the condition of the physical body, one can still tune in to the things of the spirit, and still recognise divine ideas. This then clearly lights up those opportunities for so called older people, for they have learnt from longer experience to give of the very essence of their souls; to radiate love and light; to give encouragement and knowing when to speak and when to keep silent.

A great point of importance is the need to continue and carry forward a rhythm of service and spiritual living, in order that when one is free from the limitations of the physical body and standing on the inner side of the veil, there should be no gap in the pattern of service that has been established. Life must be a continuing experience where all of one's present efforts are not lost, but are in fact seen as part of a process which flows from one life to another.

So as life proceeds, and we eventually and inevitably face the disbanding of our earthly bodies, we are really challenged to face up to our knowledge of the spirit. Spirit work is essentially an inner work and work that is done from behind the scenes of things. As we reflect on these things it conditions our inner development, thus making us better able to act as anchors through which the power of the spirit can flow into the earth's thought atmosphere, from whence it may influence the deeper thinkers of the world who are responsible for bringing about changes.

With renewed endeavour, enlightened understanding and courage, go forth in the service of spirit, ever remembering that they stand behind every effort. On that point, have no doubt! They shield and protect, leaving us free to work as we see fit.

29. THY KINGDOM COME........ON EARTH

Christ came to bring into being upon earth that which we have come to call the Kingdom of God. He came to show men what is outer and constantly changing, and that which is inner and has true meaning and reality. He revealed this inner world of meaning in order that men no longer need question the nature of God. He demonstrated the values of this world in his own life, portraying for us the character of its citizenship.

Love, brotherhood, service, recognition of the good in all things - these are the characteristics of the citizen of the Kingdom, and these still remain the ideals. Therefore, the question facing mankind today is just what can be done to bring about those objectives which Christ held before us. How can we materialise on earth that state of consciousness accompanied by that condition of living, the result of which would deserve to be recognised as being of the Kingdom of God?

Christ said that man is divine and a son of the Father. Then let us proceed to express that divinity and claim that birthright. In the life of Christ we have the complete example of that divinity that lived on earth, and lived, as most of us have to live it, not in remote retirement, but in the full storm and stress of life. He blazed the trail and is still waiting for us to follow like the children of Israel under Moses; we must go out and find the "Holy Land"; to find that which is deeper and more fundamental than sexuality or the craving for social status and deeper than the desire for mere possessions. There is a deeper craving in the human make-up, and it is the craving for knowledge. Knowledge of the right kind: the truth. Now how can we train ourselves into that right kind of knowledge? Can it be answered by following the guidance of the inner Christ? By obeying that Inner Light which we all have, and which makes us all sensitive to inspiration from high? We have no excuse for failing, for others have gone ahead and Christ kept pointing it out, making it clear and simple.

Obedience to the highest one knows in small things, as well as the great seems on the face of it too simple a rule for many to follow. They demand so much more. Yet when a simple rule is given, being told merely to obey the voice of conscience, there is not enough interest to call forth a prompt response. But this was the first rule, which Christ followed when as a child he said he came to do his father's business. He followed step by step the inner voice and it led him from Bethlehem to Calvary. It took him further; it took him through the resurrection to the mount of ascension. Thus he showed to us what results stem from obedience to the inner call, and also showed us what God in man could do and should be.

The 'achieving' is not a simple matter of building a good character and being nice and kind; more than that is involved. It is a question of understanding a new inner attitude to life that is different to the usual positions of ordinary outer living. An inner attitude is attuned to the spirit within and is itself attuned to the service of mankind. Self-knowledge leads to God knowledge. We are human beings, but we are also divine. We are citizens of the kingdom of God and his inspiration is pouring in all the time. Love is latent in every heart. Only obedience to the voice within is required as a first step, and when that is rendered in service which is an expression of love, it becomes a definite part of life. This is what Christ came to reveal; to show our human as well as our divine possibilities. By accepting the fact of our divine nature, we can begin to aid in the founding of the Kingdom on Earth -"Thy Kingdom come, on Earth, as it is in Heaven".

30.   "LIFE MORE ABUNDANT"(St. John. X. 10)

Jesus said that he had come to give life and to give it more abundantly. He then followed that statement by saying that as the "Good Shepherd" He would lay down His life for us, His sheep. It has therefore come about that men have always seen a special meaning and connection in the death of Jesus, and in the bringing of "Life more abundant" to mankind.

Now in turning our attention to the story of the Crucifixion, it is obvious that there is no need to recount the details; they are so well known. The tale of Christ gathering with his disciples in the upper room, there to share in the bread and wine before being betrayed, tried, crucified, and deserted by those who supposedly loved him, is very familiar to all. And here is the true tragedy of it all: That he did so much, and we have understood so little; he spent His life demonstrating how to serve mankind. In His teachings he brought forward continuously how to lead the spiritual life in order that we may know "The Kingdom of God" . This was His whole theme, and we have largely ignored it, because we have emphasised the personality of Jesus Christ: The one theme that He Himself ignored as being of small importance in view of the greater values that He was trying to show to the people. This again is the true tragedy of the Christ. He had one set of values, and mankind has lived by another.

The Churches have made of the Crucifixion a great story of Christ's suffering in order to save the world. But surely, His true suffering would lie in the fact that the whole meaning of His life has not been understood. The people have not been able to see what really will 'Save" them is that expression of Love for all mankind that Christ so demonstrated through His whole life. His sufferings were based upon His unique vision, of how this Love could bring all the people to literally be able to experience nothing less than God Himself. The full spiritual Life. This is the "Life more abundant" that He spoke of. This "Life more abundant" is not a life to be lived in a hereafter, in some distant Heaven, where those who are believers shall enjoy an exclusive life of happiness, while the rest of God's children are left outside.

Now, the Cross is surely intended to indicate to us how this Kingdom of God can be experienced on earth. It stands as the sign of the "I" crossed out, the self or ego being put in its proper place. It stands as the picture of a man with arms outstretched towards humanity in blessing, while He himself is on the borderline between the physical and the spirit worlds. It is when we adopt this attitude to life, of being one with the spirit while yet facing the world, and in that attitude crossing out the "Self", that we will be able to understand a little bit better what the "Greater Life" is all about. That "Life more abundant" which Christ so demonstrated in the most complete life that the world has ever seen, and which was acted out for us in that strange land which is a narrow strip between two hemispheres, again showing to us that this "Life more abundant" is only experienced when our attitude to life is standing between two worlds: the world of spirit and the physical world. The effort to carry out that perfect life in expressing the complete will of God, provoked so much antagonism that it sent Christ to the Crucifixion, something that had been foreseen and for which He was prepared. It was the hardness of men's hearts, and the weakness of their love, that brought this about. Above all, it occurred through a failure to see the vision of a "Life more abundant".

It is time that men and women of goodwill everywhere came to see Christ's true message, which is that the life of God and God's Kingdom, as it is called , can be experienced here and now on earth. People are no longer interested in a possible heavenly state somewhere in a remote future. They need to learn that it is here and that it is up to all of us to express it on earth. It is expressed by those who do the will of God; the will to do good, at all costs, as Christ did, and to demonstrate a love for one another as Christ demonstrated to us. The whole way to express the "Kingdom of Heaven " is by following Christ's pattern, as that was the full expression of his life. That was by forgetting the personal self completely as one becomes concerned for the good of the world, and by serving others instead of serving oneself.

31.   LOVE IN PRACTICE

The world stands today at a point of great tension and seemingly dangerous situations. Great divisions within the family of men are revealing the basic infancy of the soul of men; and an inability to understand and handle the laws of the spirit within which they work and have their very being.

Today mankind has developed the mind and the mental capacity for experiment, experience, and expression to a brilliant zenith, and he is searching out towards a sense of purpose, and direction for a realisation of the goals to be achieved, as a setting for those subtler realms which his searchings are beginning to reveal. In so doing he is overlooking the immediate world of meaning, quality, and inner values to which his knowledge could be dedicated. The student of the spirit knows that relating this mass of intelligent activity, with the power and will of God's purpose, must be the principle of love, which alone could give meaning and quality to any knowledge, and also wisdom as to indicate what we do with that knowledge. This relating factor of love is something to be searched for whenever there appears a crisis within the life of an individual man or within the race of men, for here alone will be found that balance between what is known in the immediate outer conditions, and what could be known from the meaning and purpose behind such activity. For men do not love enough; hence the imbalance in the use of power and wealth which generates so much hatred and darkness across the world.

How can you co-operate to help bring right choices, right decisions, and right progress to suffering humanity? How can you give of what you have and no one else can give? For although men do work increasingly in group formation, each individual is unique in the contribution he has to make. Like the thumbprint, no one person is exactly like another, and the contribution of each one is needed to the total group effort. Humanity lives and moves in groups, and today you are experiencing a simultaneous process of spiritual growth to coincide with man's increasing control of his physical environment. You are being presented with the opportunity to express to an extent greater than you have yet succeeded in doing, the power, the love, and the inclusiveness of the ONE SOUL... for all souls of men are one ...so that you may begin to function in world affairs as one humanity.

What is this love? It is so difficult to define that usually one finds oneself reduced to the negative way of 'it is not this, and it is not that, 'it is not sentiment; it is not devotion or emotion, it is not feeling nor is it attachment; it is certainly not a demand to be loved. Essentially, and greatly oversimplified, we might say that love is relationship, that experience of at-onement and sense of non-separateness which is of the life and nature of the soul. It epitomises that relationship between man and man when you can experience a concern for a Red Guard in China as you would for the welfare of one in your own family, and through this caring and understanding of your relationship with all other men, you begin to understand the relationship between man and God. The fusing of these two relationships must see the bursting forth into light of that great mediator: the Christ- like love that was so perfectly demonstrated by the Master Jesus. The power of the Christ can literally flow and be experienced in everyday forms of service, whatever they may be.

But in the meantime you have to take those steps that will help you realise the immediate goal of a heart infused with the life of the Christ. They are the steps that call you to enter into the stream of spiritual life bringing your stamp of compassion and understanding, so that you might join with the forces of light in bringing about the healing of so much that is torn apart. These steps help transform knowledge into wisdom and establish the right relationship between the peoples of the world so that mankind can safely transfer into the new age that is dawning.

32. MEDITATION

Meditation is a reflective attitude of mind that one carries around in the aura of one's self, whereby a person is constantly open to impressions that are conditioning the life of the human family. Prolonged concentration upon some form or other becomes meditation which, when carried on beyond the form and into the spirit (from whence the form finds its life) passes into contemplation. Meditation is the source of inspiration and illumination. This opens a psychic door, thus producing a flow of spirit forces, conditioned upon the motives and colouring of your own personality. So you begin to register the "Things of the spirit" and acquire the facility to penetrate into the world of meaning.

It is through meditation in one form or another that contacts are made. Be they the idea of the un-spiritual man to make a contact with that which leads him to a betterment of his daily life in a material sense, or the selfless spiritual man seeking contact with God the Father, in order to condition his daily life according to the Divine Plan. It might also be said that it is meditation which is responsible for transforming the desires of the ordinary human beings into the Spiritual will to do good. It is meditation that is the divine prompter that fuses and blends emotional desires with clear thinking into a conscious identification with the soul and Spirit of man.

One can trace many grades of meditation conditioning life on earth today. First there is just plain desire for some sort of attainment in the world from the lowest physical desires to the longings of the aspirational mystic, which are nevertheless a longing to achieve in this world . Then comes that stage of meditation called prayer. This is the stage where the aspirational mystic and the religiously inclined man blends his lower gross desires with the higher desires for a Godly relationship, and contact. He discovers through the power of prayer the subtler powers of the spirit, even if it is only to become aware that he has a higher and lower self. Then we see the mental reflection produced by concentrated thinking. This has led to the scientific mind, which has produced all the wonders of modern civilization. Finally, we can gather all the desires, prayers and deep thoughts into a balanced attitude, which produces that soul infused person where all emotions, desires and thoughts are in perfect harmony with the Soul and Spirit.

All these expressions of meditation, whether of physical desires or Spiritual aspirations, do definitely create that which is desired. These stages are responsible for all that is seen, possessed, utilized and known in the tangible world. Mankind has inherited from previous civilizations the fruits of their concentrated meditations consciously or unconsciously; much has been of value but much has proved disastrous in nature. In their turn men today create the coming civilization, and taken as a whole we can trace the stages of meditation in the mass of men.

First there is worship. This is the united recognition of men of the divine presence reflecting in humanity. It is implemented by the world religions, and creates a path of return to the source of divine life. Then there is that mass form of meditation, where men and women in every land strive towards an uplift of mankind. Unknown to each other, they are yet united in their common desire in working to create a new world order based on more spiritual values. Finally, you have those powerhouses of spiritual forces based on the creating of a channel of contact between man and spirit, so as to bring about those conditions where God's purpose might find expression, and be recognised and manifested on earth. Prayer and worship underline this recognition of spirit potency. The meditative attitude penetrates that which lies beyond all surface things into the very livingness of all, and in doing so, carries the great process of redemption a little further, of which the life of Christ was the symbol, the guarantee and the eternal testimony.

33. "MY PEACE I GIVE UNTO YOU: NOT AS THE WORLD GIVETH"
John 14. 27

There is a lot of confusion in the mind over the question of peace. What kind of peace should we work for? The peace we should not work for is that sleepy tranquil peace where nothing happens. That is the peace that can be found in a stagnant pool. We must beware of thinking of peace as something static. Love for mankind can involve us in fighting righteous wars for others, as Christ himself said "I came not to send peace, but a sword" (Matthew 10, 34.)

Peace then can be seen as the opposite of change, but obviously we should work for change that is in harmony with the spirit of evolution. Change is one sure fact of life. The peace then we should be working for is not a cause but an effect. What we should be interested in is how to bring about the effect of peace, not by being a pacifist but by learning about the true nature of peace and how to achieve it.

What is peace? It is essentially the establishing of right human relations, of a united rapport and understanding, with its resulting cooperation. What we should be trying to do is to bring about this right relationship between people by the practice of intelligent goodwill, for goodwill is the active principle of peace. Basic to understanding goodwill is the recognition of cooperation and an open mind to see the other person's point of view. Here is where our work should be, not with the effect of peace, but with the cause - goodwill.

Now we are all one humanity and that brings us to the recognition that 'Souls of men are one' for it is first and foremost as spiritual beings that we are one human brotherhood. Recognition of this true brotherhood of man, based on the divine life working through each soul and through all humanity, directs us to the further relationship of all mankind, to the vaster divine life we call God. Then men might view goodwill as being an expression of Godwill or God's will. It is this kind of developing spiritual attitude that will lead to right human relationships and eventually to peace. It is realisation which will achieve the ultimate objective of peace, not through putting peace first, but by putting first the realisation of the true unity of the whole, and of the cooperating in the distribution of the energies of that one life.

Those energies are within each one of us and are the reflection of the spark of the divine life that is in each of us. That reflection of the peace of God is not a quality which we acquire, but it is a power that we release. By meditation upon light and radiance and by learning of the spirit within man this power can be released. A power which 'Maketh all things new.' It lives and moves in those who know themselves as one with all life, and has been described as the peace that passeth understanding.

34.   BECOME AS THE CHRIST

Students of the spiritual life learn and grow by living the life of service to their fellow men. We learn by doing and we grow by basing our actions and our attitudes on what we accept as possible and reasonable, in the light of our understanding of the laws of the spirit.

Sooner or later we come to a point where we realise that the gaps in our understanding are closing, and new perspectives emerge which continue through future stages of growth, to act as a balancing and stabilising influence for identifying spiritual realities in any new situation. The teachings that one has received, and one's response to them, begin to fall into place. Then it is that aggressive individuality begins to modify, recede, and to blend with an underlying plan affecting others. The realisation of personal accomplishment recedes into the background until it fades out altogether, and one begins to realise that we are simply channels and instruments where-by the spirit of good may reach humanity, so bringing to mankind fresh life and energy. Thus is manifest and demonstrated the spirit of the Christ, which is present in each individual man and woman.

To strive to become like the Christ seems on the face of it, an impossible dream. Yet this is the goal and vision for mankind as a whole, and the least of us may cooperate with this vast purpose once we open ourselves to accept this ultimate possibility. The Christ is not an unknowable, intangible power, but is a man, having known within himself, the human characteristics that make for weakness and folly, bearing also within himself the same spark of divine fire; that eternal spirit of God, which ensouls every human being and which lies dormant within every human heart.

The Christ is both perfected man and manifested God charged with a service to both God and man. The manifestation of his spirit is therefore a divinely guaranteed objective, an incentive to men and the living substance from which mankind will evolve his own contribution to the life of God. That man can cooperate in this process is dependant on the recognition that he is indeed 'Made in the image of God' and that the law of Christ; to love God, and to love your neighbour as yourself, is the key that opens the door into a phase of growth - experience and useful service, applicable to any human situation in any part of the suffering globe.

If we look at the life of Christ in Palestine, as it has been recorded, we find the phenomena of both spiritual and material effects flowing from his words and deeds. He established a doctrine based on the divine principle and law of love. He revealed this law of love as the law from which all others stem, and he showed the way into the "Kingdom of Heaven" as lying within the heart and soul of man. At the same time, he healed the sick, fed the hungry and cared for the poor, the outcast, and the sinner.

As a new age is being inaugurated, the work he established must be continued. The work to lift humanity in consciousness, to increase human freedom and well-being and to implement the principle of love as the most powerful force in the universe. In so working, the spiritual life of man, freed from the weight of material preoccupations, will begin to blossom and intensify in beauty and radiance. Humanity as a whole will then move towards a realisation that there is a guiding force, a supreme intelligence behind the affairs of man and that it is our common destiny to become at one with its purpose and plan.

Here then is the opportunity provided and the hope of the future. The central problem today is to "Lay hold upon our divinity and make it manifest". To reveal Christ in the human heart. The Christ most perfectly a man in his divine identity with God.

Conscious of these things we can understand, we need to be practical , persistent and enduring in the face of discouragement, knowing that the spirit in man can triumph. Look for the spirit of Christ in those who serve with self-forgetfulness and harmlessness. Support and strengthen their efforts when, where and whatever way is within our power, so that together we may strive to bring in the age of brotherhood, peace, and goodwill.

35.   EVOCATION

The world today is more spiritually inclined than it has ever been. This is said in the full realisation of the generally accepted view that man is on the rocks spiritually. But this point of view is only held because of the fact that the people are not very interested in the orthodox presentation of truth, and because the churches are relatively empty. In point of fact, human beings everywhere are searching for spiritual understanding and a meaning to life. Today, people everywhere are ready for some light and there is a general air of expectation for a new dispensation. They are ready because humanity has advanced so far along the way of evolution, and it shows in their demands and what they expect out of life. No more are these being couched just in terms of material betterment, but also in terms of true values to life, wanting some meaning to life, and in some spiritual vision in the search for better human relations.

Surely then we can conclude that this increasing spiritual demand must have attracted the attention of those higher masters on the spirit side of life, for humanity is in a desperate need and that need must be met. God has never left the world without a witness, and there has never been a time when there was not the offer of some teaching, and some spiritual help in response to human need. Never have human hearts and minds gone out to God, but that divinity itself came nearer to man.

Men call forth a response from divinity in various ways. There is that undeveloped, voiceless appeal wrung from the hearts of men in all times of distress and trouble. This crying appeal rises ceaselessly from all men living under the stress and strain of life on earth, and is generally addressed to that power outside of themselves which they feel can, and should come to their aid. That it is mostly ineffectual is due to the fact that it is chiefly uncontrolled, not thought out, and self-centred.   Revolving around the "I" it travels no further.   Then there is that planned, controlled calling of spiritually-minded thinkers, who gather in groups, to give of their power and direction to the spirit powers, thus creating a line of contact for the closer approach of those higher masters who serve mankind.

The science of calling forth these higher powers must take the place of what is now called "prayer" and "worship". (Don't be disturbed by the use of the word "Science" for it is not the cold and heartless intellectual thing it is so often made out to be). This new work of calling forth the divine powers from on high must surely form the basis of any coming world religion. This new science of religion, for which prayer, meditation and ritual have prepared mankind, will train the people to present a controlled and voiced demand for a closer relationship with God and with each other. This work, when rightly carried out, will evoke a response from the waiting masters on the spirit side of life, and from their head, THE CHRIST. Then through this response the beliefs of the masses will gradually change into the conviction of those who know, and men will be transformed into co-workers with God in bringing into fruition the Kingdom of God on earth, in deed and in truth.

Churchmen, everywhere, need to remember that the human spirit is greater than all the churches and greater than all their teachings. In the long run the human spirit will defeat them and proceed triumphantly into that kingdom of God, leaving them behind unless they enter as a humble part of the mass of men. Nothing under heaven can arrest the process of the human soul on its long pilgrimage from darkness into light, from the unreal into the real, from ignorance into wisdom. If the great organised religious groups in every land and composing all faiths do not offer true spiritual guidance and help, humanity will find another way. Nothing can keep the spirit of man from God.

36.   THOUGHTS ON "GOOD FRIDAY"

In considering the story of Jesus upon the Cross it is essential that we look at it in broad and general terms. Then it is surely evident that He did not die in order that you and I might go to heaven, but that He died as the result of the very natural life of service which He rendered, and because He told men to live as sons of God when He said "He that loseth his life for my sake, shall find it" - a fact in life which when closely studied is seen to lead us not to death, but the subsequent resurrection, symbolising as it did the formation of a new kind of human being, spiritualised and free from the fear of death.

Let us search briefly for what transpired when Christ died on the cross. He rendered up the earthly body part of Himself and identified Himself with the Father God. Surely He died the death of the cross to show us a picture form that the inner spirit can truly express itself when man's physical outlook on life has died, died in order to release the Christ-like spirit hidden within. The lower carnal nature must die in order that the higher divine nature may show forth in all its beauty. Christ had to die in order that, once and for all, mankind might learn the lesson, that by giving up the human nature, the divine aspect might be saved. It is only in this sense that we can talk of him dying in order that we might be saved.

Mankind has been so preoccupied with the subject of sin that he has forgotten his divinity. The Christian age has been one of mental unfoldment, and also one where great emphasis has been laid on sin and wrongdoing. The mind produces the power to analyse and observe, so with mental development has come a growing sense of doing wrong, which has produced an almost abject attitude of an inferiority complex to the creator. This could be described as the negative side of the recognition of how much man has yet to go in understanding the ways of the creator, a recognition of the greatness of God. Against this sense of sin with its attitude of atonement in the blood of Christ there is today a revolt, for men can never get too far from divinity. Theology has over-reached itself with the "miserable sinner" complex, and its redemption in the 'Blood of Christ'. Who can say that it is not this realisation, dim and uncertain as it may be, which prompts the present universal unrest and widespread determination to better conditions? That this interpretation is in terms of the material is inevitable at first ;but it is a hopeful and spiritual sign that mankind is today busy cleaning his house, and thus attempting to raise the level of civilisation.

When men lay the emphasis of their living upon the living Christ, we shall have the emergence of a new age religion, when men will be able to say as Christ said on the cross "It is finished". Old ways of thought, the miserable sinner complex, the blood of Christ's atonement; the hold of the lower nature - all these will be finished. Individual salvation is surely a selfish outlook. We must serve one another in order to be saved, and we can only serve intelligently if we believe in the divinity of all men, all being sons of the Father. The kingdom of heaven is a kingdom of servers of the race. Love is the beginning and Love is the end. In Love we can serve and work. So surely the long pilgrim's progress will end in the glory of the giving up of all the lower personal desires, and merging all one's being in the living spirit that is to be found in and through all things.

Hibiscus

37. RESURRECTION

When life seems hard and circumstances carry no grounds for happiness, the thought of rising up and out of these circumstances into a new life carries with it a certain strength and hope. This basic thought reaches its highest expression at Easter, the day of the resurrection. Christ by His resurrection proved that there was no death. He demonstrated to us the meaning of the divine life that was present in Him and in all of us. Christ conquered death because it is innate in all humanity to do so, and Christ alive today in every human heart is the guarantee of the divinity of mankind.

When men know themselves as divine, then they will know themselves as immortal, and so recognise death as the prelude to further living experience, bringing with it release and a setting free. This in turn must bring the thought that there is a purpose in life far greater than the petty aims of caring for a body and educating a mind, though they have their place. Life cannot be a futile process of aimless wandering, but must exist to embrace the widest and highest ideals, such as ideas that are divine and worthy of carrying into immortality; ideas eternal. When we care for that which is eternal in value, then eternal life, free from the limitations of the flesh , is ours. What we really care about in our highest moments determines the quality of our immortal life. When a man's life has gained significance then he is ready to follow in the steps of Christ's example.

At some time, and in some place, we must knowingly and willing enter and work in the world of values. We must create that attitude of mind that says "I will arise and go to my Father", and so make ourselves worthy for that citizenship in the Kingdom of God. The resurrection is not the rising of the dead from their tombs, but is the passage from the death of selfish living into the life of unselfish love. Only through love can the real message of the Christ be understood, for it is love which penetrates to the heart of reality, and has the faculty of discovering the truth that is hidden behind the form. The resurrection, therefore, might be defined as that persistence into the future of all that which is divine; the rising of all the Christ-like qualities in human nature and human society are presented in a fuller, higher and richer mode of expression. This resurrection is going on continuously. The divine spirit is always rising within mankind. The stone of matter is always being rolled away from the tombs of confining life in order that the Divine within may come forth in glory and its power.

Hence it is that we witness the world today in a great confusion of re-adjustments, of striving and struggling. Let us try to understand the upheaval and chaos as one of mankind breaking out of the tombs of selfishness and individual gain, and coming into the living light and basic unity, so facing towards the real values of life. Let us then penetrate into the darkness with what light we have, and see humanity stirring as spiritual strength and life increase in the race of men. We are privileged to be present at this moment of stress for all mankind, for we are seeing the birth of a new and deathless race, a race in which the germ of immortality will flower, and in which divinity can express itself through the race of men. That which is of everlasting value is coming to the fore. It has always been there, but today it can be seen ushering in the great message of Christ's ministry. Namely, that immortality does not begin after death, but is a continuous development of spiritual activity in a life of service given to one's fellow men. So we may lose sight of our individual personalities, but instead, express something of value to God and man. This surely is the true resurrection. The rising in order to go to the Father because a noble life is worth having.

38. CHRISTMAS

In coming to Earth and taking human incarnation God testified his faith in the divinity which is in man. God had sufficient confidence in man that he sent forth his Son to demonstrate the possibilities to man. It was man's divinity that warranted such an expression. So God acted. God had such faith in man's innate spirituality that he ventured on a great mission that led into the Christian experience, Faith in Christ ! Faith in mankind! Faith in man's responsiveness to transmute the vision into experience.

The Christian faith, in spite of dogma and distortion, has done a great deal to bring God and man together. This vital yet living truth when grasped by the mind and understood by the heart, should enable all seekers after truth to have faith to venture and experience a new birth into light and truth.

One of these truths is that the love of God is eternal, and that His love for his people has been steadfast and unalterable. Whenever the time is ripe and the need of the people warrants it, He comes forth for the guidance of man. Again and again such teachers have come forth and manifested as much of the divine nature as the development of mankind has warranted, spoken those words which have determined the culture and civilization of a time, and then passed on their way, leaving the seed to germinate and bear fruit.

So it was that in the fullness of time Christ came. He came because the world of men drew him, and the love of the Father impelled him. He came to give life a purpose and fulfilment and to indicate to us the way. He came to give us an example, which is to say that when we are Christ-1ike, then we shall have peace on Earth and goodwill among men. When this has taken place, the glory of God will be seen. It is only when we are expressing the divinity within us that hatred will break down and goodwill steps in. When there is goodwill, there must be peace. When there is peace, we can plan more confidently for the future. The future of good will is God's will, and the future of God's will must surely be seen in Christ who was God and Man. The future then is always towards drawing together the qualities of God and the qualities of man.

The life of God is today agitating the minds of men, and causing them to move towards a newer world, where higher ideals and deeper contacts might be made possible.

39.   VALUES TO LIVE BY

The fate of men and nations is determined by the values which govern their decisions.

The present era is laden with dangers and opportunities unprecedented in human history. However, when one observes man's response to this era of crisis, then his purposes, priorities, attitudes and values seem almost absurd, having little relevance to the fundamental issues of realities of the times.

Were there to be a major war, mankind could be destroyed. Yet nations now spend millions on offensive armaments. Furthermore, the relation between the power of an elite handful of nations and the well-being of the rest of humanity is so imbalanced that, should a major war arise, the people of all nations might be sacrificed for the interests of this fractional percentage of humanity.

Distorted priorities and values are also evident in the widening gap between rich and poor nations. While developed nations experience prosperity, two-thirds of mankind experience a malnutrition, which can permanently impair their life expression. While there are the technological resources to provide physical security for all humanity, calls for co-operation in international development meet only with polite gestures.

The seeming blindness of men to fundamental issues is also demonstrated in the ecology crisis. Having recognised that the planet is a finite life-supporting system, whose harmonious functioning depends on a delicately balanced ecosystem of which man is a part, still man continues to act as if he were nature's master, rather than nature's partner. In pursuit of unlimited expansion on a finite globe, he employs science and technology for the manipulation of nature and its forces, with little regard to possible consequences.

The scope of problems, which now afflict mankind and its civilisation, is awesome. Problems such as dehumanisation, over-population, illiteracy, worldwide unemployment, energy crisis and monetary problems affecting all nations can only be solved by the united effort of all the world's peoples. Within this century science and technology have rendered obsolete the age-old attitude of separatism. Each nation and individual is now linked by a web of interdependence, wherein the actions and problems of one affect the well-being of the whole. Thus with such global problems posing a common threat to all mankind, one might expect that men and nations would set aside their selfish priorities, and undertake a united and co-operative response to the quickly congealing world crisis.

Yet men and women on the individual, family, community, and national level continue to assert that the interests of the unit are not only more important, but also different from the common good of the greater whole. Their actions fall short of the needed unity of purpose and this endangers humanity's survival.

At the heart of this world crisis is a crisis of values.
Separate and selfish attitudes nurtured during ages of relative isolation have now to be challenged. Separatism, greed, competition and irresponsibility are outmoded, for they are incapable of solving the problems of new global dimensions. New values arc needed.

The major problems we face are identifiable. The means of solving them are not so obvious, but they exist. It is largely a matter of choice. If we so choose, we have the genius, the imagination, the know-how, as well as the resources to improve the quality of life for all humanity. Therefore our major problem is one of what we desire and how we decide. It is a problem of character and values, because our world crisis today derives basically from whatever values we choose to live by.

Man has distinguished himself for centuries by his selfishness, greed and aggression. These character defects, plus fear and suspicion based on a primitive instinct for survival and self perpetuation, have accounted for his warlike tendencies. So we have fear, greed, and selfishness as the basis of all violence and aggression on a local, national, and international scale, aggravated during the course of this century by materialism. The manufacture, scale, and use of all kinds of armaments are a massive industry wielding political power and influence. It has crippled our ability and stifled our will to feed, clothe, house, educate and train the needy. So interwoven with national economies and the political and social structure has this cancer become, that it successfully resists a11 direct efforts to control and reduce it to a proportion, which more equitably reflects its actual value in defence to any nation.

Therefore, since the structure itself is impregnable, we need to pay attention to the human attitudes of mind and heart which are responsible for its creation and its maintenance, including the ideologies and national goals. It is human attitudes which determine the accepted values and standards of living, and the decisions and choices which preserve and perpetuate the status quo.

Attitudes of mind and heart can change, and attitudes always precede any change in an individual, or any race, or nation. These attitudes are the consciousness factor. They reflect the principles and ideals that are accepted as a basis for living. So a time of ferment such as today is indicative of change in consciousness. It implies a rejection of those ideals and attitudes no longer acceptable as a measure of the good life, and this permits entry to ideas more in line with the needs and facts of the world today.

We might define some of these ideas in these terms:-
1)   The separatism which has characterised human life on earth for so long, can yield today in this inter-related world structure to an attitude of inclusiveness. Every thought, word and deed of each individual, group or nation has its effects on a11 other individuals, groups and nations, and therefore this must be considered at all times.

2.) The selfishness and self-interest which have determined our struggle for survival, identity and supremacy can be superseded by selflessness. This brings forward the principle of co-operation and sacrifice of self in the interest of the greater whole. Whatever is good for people everywhere is good for each one.

3.) The materialism of present man with his capacity to produce material things can be transcended by the realisation that quality in daily life is more conductive to a happy life than quantity.
A quality life is dependent on a spiritual scale of values: ethical and moral integrity, honesty, caring, concern, with a commitment to practical activities.

4.) Human behaviour has long been characterised by irresponsibility ,acting only in its own interest and ignoring the rights of others.   Responsible behaviour is the only correction. Each individual and every organisation carry a personal responsibility. The acceptance of this responsibility in small and large issues sets an infectious and irresistible example.

5.) With human society in its present condition of breaking down prior to rebuilding, reactionary cynicism is a familiar attitude of mind, and this is destructive in its effects. Man is, however, a spiritual as well as a material being.   In his innate being he is essentially divine, and the evolutionary process consists of his growing awareness of this fact.   He is, therefore, always capable of better attitudes and behaviour.   A belief in man as an inherently spiritual being and that the heart of mankind is basically sound, provides an incentive that can inspire constructive attitudes and actions.
Here therefore are five values that men can choose to live by:-

1)   INCLUSIVENESS in all thoughts and actions.
2)   SELFLESSNESS.
3)   ENHANCEMENT OF THE QUALITY OF DAILY LIFE.
4)   PERSONAL RESPONSIBILITY.
5)   BELIEF IN MAN'S POTENTIAL GOODNESS.

These are simple, practical, as well as idealistic. If sincerely understood, accepted, and practised in all walks of life, and in all societies and nations, the quality and way of life of that society or nation must change. Groups and nations consist of the individuals that comprise them. The quality of the people and the values they choose to live by determine the quality of a national life, and of the type of leadership that establishes the policies, priorities, and the objectives. In these concerns, all are involved. Right constructive values to live by are a practical means of producing a quality way of life for the race of men.

40. THE ETHERIC BODY

The soul pours its directed energy into the physical body through the medium of the etheric or vital body. This etheric body has been described as a network permeated with fire, or as a web animated with golden light. It is composed of that matter which we call etheric and its shape is brought about by the fine interlacing strands of this matter being built into the form or mould upon which the dense physical body can be moulded. Under the law of attraction the denser matter of the physical plane is made to cohere to this vitalised form and is gradually built up around it, and within it, until the interpenetration is so complete that the two make one unit. The physical body is the direct result of the inner activity of this network.

The etheric body is the inner scaffolding which underlies every part of the whole outer man. It is the framework which sustains the whole. It is a network of nadis, infinitely intricate, which constitutes the duplicate of the entire nervous system. It is thus with the blood stream the instrument of the life force. If, therefore, there is a weakness in the relationship between the inner structure and the outer form, it will be apparent that the real difficulty will supervene. This difficulty will take three forms:

1) The physical body is loosely connected with the etheric body leading to a de-vitalisation and debilitated condition pre-disposing a man to ill health.

2) The connection may be poor in certain focal points where the life force cannot adequately flow and therefore there is a definite weakness in some part of the body.

3) When the physical body is so closely knit with the personality that every part of the physical body is in a constant condition of stimulation with a resultant activity in the nervous system, which if not correctly regulated, can lead to a great deal of distress.

The etheric body is a potent receiver of impressions, which are conveyed to the human consciousness through the medium of awakened centres of power. These impressions and information become the incentive whereby conscious activity is begun. There are many words used to describe these activating effects, such as impulses, incentives, influences, desires, aspirations and many such terms which are all really synonyms for force or energy. All these words refer to forms of activity of the etheric body, but only when the physical body registers and acts under these impressions.

The etheric body has one main objective. This is to vitalise and energise the physical body and thus integrate it into the energy body of the earth and of the solar system. It is be remembered that the etheric body of the human being is an integral part of the etheric body of the planet and therefore related to all forms found within that body in all the kingdoms of nature. This constant circulation of life forces through the etheric bodies of all forms - human, planetary, and solar - is the basis of all manifested life and the expression of the essential non-separateness of life, and hence provides the scientific basis for unity.

The vastness of the subject and the whole theme of motivating force is so real, that only little by little can man grasp the situation, and come to realise that he is essentially, through his etheric body, an integral part of a great and vibrant whole. Only in time through the process of evolution can he hope to register all the different areas of divine expression. Only when the etheric body is swept into activity under the influence and through the "impressed forces" of the soul, the mind, and temporarily the astral or emotional body, can man become aware of all worlds, all phenomena, and all states of consciousness, and so achieve that omniscience which is the birthright of all Sons of God.

41.   THE MASS

A concept of the dynamics of energy flow, and the role of the priest in the ritual of the Catholic Mass. Five questions to be asked: What is actually happening when we take part in a church service, as at the Eucharistic Mass? What is the object in carrying out such a ritual?   What is the esoteric meaning? What is the nature of the religious experience and what is the celebrant actually doing? What is the nature of the energies inherent in the process?

"The Form of the Eucharist".

The Eucharist is a sacrificial ritual where trans-substantiation occurs. It is an ancient initiatory rite. It produces an interplay of energies and weaves them together to produce an effect. The Form of the Mass is celebrated in four stages.

1)   The Physical Form.   *(Entering)*
This stage includes the Asperge, the Confiteor, and the Absolution. The object is to purify the congregation and the space around the Altar, to ensure there is no contamination of the incoming spiritual energies by banishing any pre-existing negative energies.
The Asperge is where the priest sprinkles potentised holy water around the Altar and then to the four corners of the church. In the Confiteor the congregation open themselves up to receive the spiritual energies generated by the Mass. This part is completed by the priest giving the congregation absolution.

2)   The Emotional Form.   *(Evocation)*
The object of this stage is to evoke the emotional energies derived from the congregation. It includes the introit, the Kyrie and the Gloria. The introit opens up the emotional centres of consciousness of the congregation. The Kyrie creates an aspiration by asking God for an outpouring of his spirit. The Gloria produces an emotional peak with a massed uprising of energies at the emotional level, enhanced by the organ rising in crescendo and resonating with the emotional centres.

3)   The Mental Form.   *(Purification)*
This stage includes the Collects, the Epistle, the Gospel and the Credo. Its object is to activate the mental and creative energy centres of the congregation. The censing of the Book of the Gospels tends to stimulate the sharpness of the mind. The Collect articulates the theme of the Mass, thus producing a mental response by the congregation. The Epistle makes the connection between the congregation, the Christ impulse, and the church, through a reiteration of its historical foundation. The Gospel causes a shift

from the lower rational mind to the higher intuitive mind in order to receive its spiritual message. The Credo should not be treated as a set of dogmatic tenets, but at a deeper level it should give each person just what he or she is able to receive. It should make the congregation consider the abstract principles.

4)   The Spiritual Form   (Sanctification)

The object of this stage is to raise the consciousness of the individual to a communion with the spirit of the Christ and ultimately with God. It is the kernel of the Eucharist. A communion of humanity with God through a manifestation of the God within. The Form commences with the offertory, where the bread and wine are brought to the altar, representing firstly, the fruits of the physical nature of humanity, and secondly, of their lower emotional natures to be symbolically sacrificed that is to say, 'Given up' in order to achieve a union with God. The celebrant now seeks to draw away the emotional energies generated by the congregation, by mentally visualising the throwing out over the congregation of a net . Then, by an effort of will, he charges the bread and wine with that generated emotional energy.

5)   *(Communion)*

The next step is to invoke the assistance of the Spirit hosts to add their energies to those of the congregation opening with the phrase "Sursum Corda" - and its responses which set up a rhythmic flow between the celebrant and congregation. The Preface which follows expresses the nature of the Trinity. The positive polarity of the Father, the negative polarity of the Holy Spirit which are earthed in the principle of the Christ. The concept is further expressed in the Sanctus which follows. The Sanctus bell is rung invoking further Spirit help in the manipulation of energy flow. The congregation then greet and thank this spirit help with the Benedictus. The celebrant now states his Intent, defining how the energies, when received, will be distributed. He may have a clear objective in mind or he may submit his will to that of the divine on the use of the energies that have been generated.

A)
The consecration of the Elements is next carried out wherein a conduit is provided to connect the physical Elements with the source of Spiritual Force. The celebrant exerts his will so that the Divine life flashes through the conduit and the trans-substantiation takes place. Next follows the Acclamation which is a thanks-giving for the presence of the Christ spirit now amongst the congregation. This is the climax of the ceremony. This is followed by the raising of the Bread and Wine to demonstrate the trans-substantiation, and a bell is rung three times at the Altar. The celebrant then silently says a prayer

of protection, making a sign of the cross as he breaks the sacred Host over the   chalice.

B)   (Thanksgiving)
The Agnus Dei follows which is a plea for mercy and peace, followed by the Kiss of Peace to remove any negative energies between members of the congregation. The Act of communion then takes place with that Presence of Christ where his love is dispersed and diffused among the people, by then taking the Host and drinking of the Wine. The celebrant then consumes any remaining Wine and Host to ensure that all trans-substantiated material with its spiritual charges is used and safely accounted for.

C)
The Benediction closes down the emotional centres of the congregation and all spiritual energies generated by the Mass are dispersed for the congregation to take away with them.

D)
The final act of the Service is the "Deo Gratias", an acclamation by the congregation of the gifts of the Spirit that have just been given to them.

(Separation)

They now depart being in a 'state of Grace' and so strengthened with an inner
force which will help and sustain them through the everyday fortunes of life.

See 47 'Ritual'

"Grace" - Read: The Grace of Devotion
Chapter 15, Book 4 of "Imitation of Christ" by Thomas `a Kempis.

Notes

Original name given to the Communion was the 'Agape' meaning the 'Love Feast' in Greek.

Eucharist = Greek for Thanksgiving.

The doctrine of Trans-substantiation was officially adopted as orthodox at the Fourth Latern Council in 1215.

Confiteor = Confession

Kyrie,Eleison = Lord have mercy.   Gloria in excelsis Deo = Glory be to God on high...

Credo in unum Deum = I believe in one God....(The Nicene Creed)

Sursum Corde: Habemus ad Dominum = Let us lift up our hearts: We have raised them up to the Lord.

References: Justin, "Apology" pages 65-66   AD150
          Professor Peter Stewart, "The Science of the Sacred" 1999.

A)   Mysterium fidel = Let us proclaim the mystery of Faith
       Mortem tuam annuntiamus Domine, donec venias = We proclaim your death, Lord Jesus,
       until you come in Glory.

B)   Agnus Dei, qui tollis peccata mundi: Miserere nobis = Lamb of God, you take away the sins
       of the world; have mercy on us.
       Pax domine sit semper vobiscum = The Peace of the Lord by with you.

C)   Benedicat vos omnipotens Deus, Pater, et Filius. et Spiritus Sanctus.
= May almighty God
       bless you, The Father, and the Son, and the Holy Spirit.

D)   Deo gratias = Thanks be to God.

42.   REQUISITE STEPS FOR PEACE

Peace is a word that means so many things to so many people that it no longer has a clear meaning. People have tried to define it for a long time; maybe it's beyond a precise definition. To try to develop a clear idea of peace requires paying attention to some of the requisite conditions that will allow that state to be manifested. A world without peace is a fragmented world. That fragmentation must be examined and understood so that its opposite, which is synthesis, can also be understood.

Synthesis, the combining of separate elements to form a coherent whole, is a different word upon which to build a clear understanding. If we consider synthesis as a desirable goal, then a completely accomplished synthesis, a Great Synthesis, like Ultimate Reality, would be an ideal to which we might aspire, an ideal that is always receding before us into infinity. It is a state in which all opposites are ultimately reconciled and in which there is only unity. A unification and harmonisation of life that surrounds us is not unimaginable or unobtainable. We can actually work on developing this. We can decide what steps must be taken to work towards peace through synthesis, for peace is a reconciliation of opposing discordant forces and reconciliation is the key. All steps leading to Great Synthesis are steps of reconciliation; we must learn to recognise these steps and see how they work. How can we build these steps? Of course we must think about peace, for thinking points us in the right direction. We must also have a great yearning, for it is this yearning with our thinking that develops a striving, and striving is action. Action means acts of reconciliation. The difficult part is that these first steps are self-initiated. Great teachers may point out a direction, may describe or convince us, but it is we who must pave the way.

Knowing the goal to be a world at peace, and knowing the way to be acts of reconciling the disharmonies, to achieve a higher harmony we can examine the possibilities for action. Any act of reconciliation has to begin with 'we' before proceeding to the greater whole. If we begin with ourselves and work outwards, then we unify our inner and outer selves; we must reconcile our understanding of our past, our present and our future; we must make our material and spiritual selves as one; in daily work we must express the great laws of the universe. Labour is the measure of value upon which evolution is built. The work we do involves not only unceasing labour but also a battle. How can harmonising be a battle? How can creativity be a battle? Creation is the overcoming of chaos. It is light overcoming darkness. People assume that creation is peaceful, but how can one think of creation without mastery over the elements, without a struggle against obstacles? Our battle is the mastery over chaos. The reconciliation of opposites is not a truce between them but a struggle for balance.

There are two principles that should be accepted so that we can grow more specific about the steps that we can take. One is the concept of diversity in unity. We often meet people who advocate a uniformity of humanity as a necessary step towards peace. This would be disastrous, as it would create conditions that are static and unmoving. Currents only flow between polarities, therefore differences between human beings are the necessary ferment that keeps us moving and growing. We must resist those who advocate sameness for humanity. Unity is alive when we have diversity and is dead without it. A second harder concept to assimilate is the importance of synthesis rather than analysis as a way of dealing with the phenomena of life. We are brought up to examine, identify, label and categorise; all these are separate methods of acquiring knowledge. Every label that we accept separates us from the others, the rest of humanity. The synthesising approach, however, makes us concentrate on similarities and encourages us not to consider the differences as important. Always keep these two factors in mind, synthesis instead of analysis and recognise diversity in unity.

If truth - Absolute Truth - is infinite, i.e. beyond our grasp, how much of the truth can be obtained in all of the life that we share? Learning is by no means futile. The great free will to knowledge, to grow and experience is a striving towards synthesis. It is the striving that ultimately leads to peace. This particular goal of knowledge is elusive because it is a continuous change. Nothing is repeatable. It makes the effort for synthesis a slippery thing. Once we have learned something, we have to work with it in an attempt to harmonise it with other things, but at every moment all is different from the moment before. How do we understand the uniqueness of each moment? By learning to understand the process of change - its flow. If our goal is synthesis, then by flowing with the river of change we will affect profoundly everything we do and experience. It will make our relationships with others clear, and will enable us to perform better the work of unification. Embrace change and never fear it, and it becomes self-evident that working towards unification is working towards achieving peace. In the spirit of synthesis we should each decide what, according to our own values, is for the common good and work for it. The reconciliation of what separates into a great synthesis is the only true Peace.

"Nothing in the universe is intelligible, living, and consistent except through an element of Synthesis, in other words a spirit, or from on high"

Teilhard de Chardin. "Science and Christ"

P.57

43.   SPEAKING SILENCE

"And I will surely hide my face"(Deut. 31 -18)

This is an instruction from the Torah which should always be read as the revealed text which co-exists with the concealed (Zohar2.230b). So an instruction to 'hide my face' commands us to look behind the surface of things, and penetrate into the meaning behind the words. In this looking we are entering into a different state of consciousness, where we must first question whether we are explaining the inner meaning or merely explaining it away? The inner meaning has its sacred language which is described as 'the silence of the spirit,' bearing in mind the sacred language is from the point of view of the divine. The spoken words bring the spirit into matter. Now at that point where the silence becomes spoken, there is a point of creation. i.e. putting spirit into matter. The "speaking silence" creation is formulated by the activity we call the imagination. Here is the creation that ascends, descends, moves and stops. From the invisible it becomes the visible. The writers of the old scriptures knew this and in the Talmud we can read how Ishmael asked Akiba what his occupation was and Akiba said, "I am a scribe", to which Ishmael replied, "Be meticulous in your work for it is the work of heaven and should you omit one single letter, or add one too many, you would destroy the whole world". When the first Tabernacle was built it was said that Bezalel knew how to combine the letters with which the heavens and earth were created. In this knowledge he created a Temple. This means he created a sacred space in which we can come to understand what is hidden behind all things. So it is we are called to study the relationships of words to their sounds and vibrations. Remember in Proverbs 15:23 you are reminded of what is written, a word spoken in its proper place is a good thing *Ask what is its proper place? When we speak, our words are dissipated and do not return, but should words revolve back into their original state to fulfil their creative purpose? So it is we come to study the "Speaking Silence", the language that surely must be the bridge between the study of psychology and the sense of mysticism. A sacred language indeed.

"It is the glory of God to conceal the word; But the honour of Kings to search out a matter" (Proverbs 25:2)

*   What is the matter to search out? Is it "A word spoken in its proper place"?

44. "THINKING GLOBALLY, LIVING RESPONSIBLY"

Teilhard Conference :   31 March -2 April 2000
Theme: Towards the fourth Millennium.
Teilhard's vision:- His Credo.
I believe the universe is in evolution.
I believe evolution develops towards spirit.
I believe spirit is completed in human beings, in the personal.
I believe the supreme personal is the Cosmic Christ.

A creation necessarily expresses itself in the form of an evolution .If God creates, he can only do so by the evolutionary method .Is it a movement of disorderly or controlled impulses? Does it show signs of containing within itself a favoured axis (i.e. line of advancement) ?As seen by Charles Darwin, the favoured axis was the 'survival of the fittest.' Teilhard's research led him to suggest that 'survival of the fittest' should read 'survival of the most complex'   (i.e. from atoms to complete humans, to Universes). Complexification is a direction of evolution. A direction which Teilhard called cosmogenesis. The propensity of matter to unite into structures of greater and greater complexity, is the same tendency as that which it has to grow interiorly in consciousness and psychically. Not just in human consciousness, for consciousness exists; it is not created or produced. Thus we discover that coming into being has a direction and a purpose opening up a sea of possibilities, which today is being explored in 'Quantum Theology' which picks up from Teilhard's view of evolution asking where is the evidence? Then Quantum physics builds the notion of transformation as a process of all activity in space, of time being relative, and that the universe is a living organism, where if it had no interior subjectivity then there would be no inter-relationship or communion. All this activity brings together life forms, always for a reason displaying an ability to work together . From the recognition of these Quantum studies we now see it is not from any forces in the past that are pushing us forward, but an attraction of the future and its possibilities that draws us, and indeed the world into an expanding horizon, in which revelation takes place. Revelation being ongoing cannot be generally included into any religion or creed. Can we then consider if this attraction that pulls is a pull from the interior of all things, a pull of the spirit? is not this attraction the outstanding quality of love? So we can say Love embodies the creative evolutionary process, and our response to it is our life's responsibility - the ability to respond. If we are to behave responsibly, we must surely deepen our understanding of the evolving material which is ourselves.

"Love is the free and imaginative outflowing of the Spirit over all unexplored paths"
Teilhard De Chardin
The Future of Man. p.55

45.   DEATH   (1)

Death to the average thinking man is a point of catastrophic crisis. It is the ending of all that has been loved, familiar and desired. It is a crashing entrance into the unknown and uncertain. No matter how much faith you may have in spiritual values or how clear your thoughts are on life everlasting, there still remains a questioning and a doubt. The longing and the sense of continuity, even to the most ardent believer, rest on probability, upon an unsure foundation and upon the testimony of others.

There is no death. There is entrance into fuller life. There is freedom from the handicaps of the fleshly body. Death, if we could realise it, is one of our most practised activities. We have died many times, and shall die again and again, for death is essentially a matter of consciousness. We are one moment conscious on the physical sphere and then we withdraw to another sphere, becoming active there. It is only as long as we identify our consciousness completely with the physical, that death will hold its old fears. So, just as soon as we know ourselves to be spiritual souls and can learn to identify our consciousness or awareness with the spiritual realms, we shall no longer know what death is.

The fear and morbidness which the subject of death usually evokes, with the unwillingness to face it with understanding, is due to the heavy emphasis that people lay upon the physical body and all things physical. It is based on an innate fear of loneliness and the loss of what is familiar. Yet the loneliness of death is as nothing compared with the loneliness of birth. At birth a spirit finds itself in new surroundings and immersed in a body, which at first is totally incompetent to take care of itself, or to establish intelligent contact with surrounding conditions. Man comes into incarnation with no recollection as to the identity or significance to him of the other people with whom he finds himself in a relationship. After death this is not so, for he finds himself on the other side of the veil with those whom he knew and had connections with. You are also conscious of those still in the physical body and can see them and tune into their thoughts and emotions, the physical brain no longer acting as a deterrent. If people but knew more; birth would be the experience most to be dreaded, and not death, for birth establishes the spirit in a true prison, while death is the first step to freedom.

46.   THE SECRET TEACHING

There is a widespread and popular idea that there is no such thing as a secret teaching in connection with Christianity. It is necessary, therefore, first to prove clearly that in the early Church at least, Christianity possessed a hidden side and that it guarded, as a priceless treasure, the secrets which were revealed only to a select few. But before doing this, it would be well to consider the whole question of this hidden side of religion, and to see why such a side must exist if a religion is to be strong and stable. If thus, its existence in Christianity will appear as a foregone conclusion, and the references to it in the writings of the early fathers will appear simple and natural, instead of surprising and intelligible.

The first question we have to answer is - what is the object of religions?
They are given to the world by men wiser than the masses of the people on whom they are bestowed and are intended to quicken human evolution. Now all men are not at the same level of evolution. The most highly evolved are far above the least evolved both in intelligence and character. It is, therefore, useless to give all the same religious teaching.   What would help the intellectual would be entirely unintelligible to the unintelligent;   on the other hand, the teaching suitable to help the unintelligent would be intolerably crude to the philosopher, while that which redeems the criminal is useless to the saint.   Yet all need religion so that each may reach upward to a life higher than that to which he is heading, and no type or grade should be sacrificed to any other.   Religion must be graduated as evolution, else it fails in its objectives.

Next comes the question - in what way do religions seek to quicken human evolution? Religion seeks to evolve the moral and intellectual nature and to aid the spiritual nature to unfold itself, with regard to man as a complex being. They seek to meet him at every point of his constitution. Teaching, therefore, must be adequate to the mind and heart to which they are addressed. Religion then takes hold of human nature and trains it, strengthens it, purifies it, and guides it towards its proper ending - the union of the human spirit with the divine so that "God may be all in all" (1 Cor. XV .28)

Looking then at Religion, and considering its object, its meaning, its origin, the nature and varying needs of the people to whom it is addressed, recognising the evolution of spiritual, intellectual, and moral faculties in man, and the need of each man for such training as is suitable for the stages of evolution at which he has arrived, we are led to the absolute necessity of a graduated religious teaching that will meet its different needs and help each man in his own place.

46a.   THE HIDDEN SIDE OF CHRISTIANITY

The New Testament and the writings of the early church make the same declarations as to the possession by the church of such teaching. Certain passages in the New Testament would remain obscure, if it were not for the light thrown on them by the definite statements of the early Fathers and Bishops.

Origen referred to a secret teaching when describing "Unto you is given to know the mystery of the Kingdom of God, but unto them that are without, all these things are done in parables" (St. Mark IV 11) . Other references in the bible include Matth.X111 11 & 34& 35. Luke V111 10.

St Paul speaks in exactly the same sense: - "We speak the wisdom of God in a mystery, even the hidden wisdom, which God ordained before the world" (Cor. 2 - 7) Paul passed his hidden knowledge to Timothy - "O Timothy keep that which is committed to thy Trust"(Tim. V1. 20).   Not the knowledge commonly possessed by Christians, for that would have had special obligation.

The early writings of those who were instructed by the first masters   who carried on with these references to a hidden teaching include:

Polycarp - Bishop of Smyrna:	The Epistle of Polycarp Ch.X11
Ignatius of S.John:	The Epistle of Ignatius to the Ephysiens.
Barnabas:	The Epistle of Barnabas Ch.1
S.Clement of Alexandria:	Stromata Bk.1 Ch.X11
Origen:	Agamst Celsus Vol.X
Maximus, the Confessor:	AD 580 - 622
Bernard of Clairvaux:	AD 1091 - 1153
Thomas Aquinas:	AD 1227 - 1274
Meister Eckhart:	AD 1260 - 1329
Thomas `a Kempis	AD 1380 - 1471
Jacob Bohme	AD 1575 - 1624
Mme de Guyon	AD 1648 - 1717
Henry More	AD 1614 - 1687
William Law	AD 1686 - 1761
S. Martin	AD 1743 - 1803

Cardinal Newman recognised a secret tradition handed down when he said "This secret tradition was authoritatively divulged and perpetuated in the creeds of the early Councils"

Brief as this outline is, it is sufficient to show the existence of a hidden side in the teaching of Christianity. Does the Church of today take up this teaching? Surely on the answers to the question depends the future of Christianity.

47.   RITUAL

To many people ritual means a childish game of dressing up and make believe. To others it is an enjoyable and dignified escape from real life. But surely it can also be one of mankind's many roads into the true life, a means of linking the spiritual with the physical. When you impose a rhythm on your life, you call it a discipline. Extend this to groups and you have a united rhythm or undertaking that is indeed a ritual. No one on earth can evade ritual, however loudly they may protest that it is not for them. The rising and setting of the sun imposes a ritual on your life, as does the passing of the years. Mankind's own inventions carry on the process. Trains, ships, and aeroplanes all operate to timetables, and thereby compel the traveller to a time ritual. Factory and school hours all contribute to the imposition of a rhythm, so helping to create a rhythm of living.

Rituals are of many types and kinds.   There are solemn ceremonies associated with religious services.   These are usually extremely formal involving vestments, chants and prayers. They have a part to play in making people recognise that spiritual powers can be called to the aid of mankind. Other rituals are more simply the efforts of those seeking to bring a rhythmic discipline in order that their lives may conform to some sensed purpose; a means whereby they try to see and understand the reality behind all things. This is a long and slow road of trying to extend one's experience of life and so put a value to it.

Today a lot of impatient people seek to hasten this extension of experience by the use of drugs.   Now why are these people so concerned with penetrating areas of perception, which lie beyond the normal reach of mind and sense? Is this not possibly a sign that the spirit of mankind as a whole is stirring, and in so doing is driving some of its human units into a search for a purpose and meaning to life.   The use of drugs is a measure of some people's impatience, allied to ignorance.   There is no quick and easy way. True extra-sensory perception represents an enlargement of the field of awareness arising from an inner enfoldment.

This inner enfoldment is the revealing of the essential spirit qualities in men and women whereby they convert the power of Good into a pattern of life, which loves service.   Seen thus, all the daily activity becomes a ritual of necessary transforming the commonplace to reveal love, beauty and the divine. All this makes it clear that ritual is not a means of providing a setting for a faith or a philosophy, but it is a means of bringing down spirit power to help in uplifting and enlightening mankind. It can be the means of making possible the divine potential within human limitations. Being these things, it can prop up the weary souls and strengthen those in need. It is the tangible intangible, which enables a man to cling with hands he hasn't got to a support that isn't there. For he is acting as if power flowed through them and in so doing, a miracle always happens. The power does flow. The strength does come. The light does shine. Somehow the character of the ritual changes and it becomes what is essentially is - a means to an end: the soul's path to the source of its being, the link between man and God and the bridge home to the Father.

Buttercup

48.   GOD'S PLAN FOR US

Looking at the physical activities taking place in the world today, it must be extremely difficult for the average intelligent person to discern the working out of a divine plan. You may be intuitively aware of a plan, but what is also needed is that ability and skill to present it to humanity in a recognisable way that will encourage them to co-operate with this plan.

The first vital factor to be communicated is that God has a plan for humanity and this plan has always existed. Generally speaking this plan is concerned with those means that will raise and expand the consciousness of mankind, enable them to discover the spiritual values for themselves, and then to make the needed changes of their own free will. When a sculptor looks at a block of stone, he sees not what must be added, but that which needs to be chipped away. We are in a somewhat similar position. We are called, not to add to the hidden reality that we sense as beyond or within, but to strip away the illusions which are preventing it being seen. The real is there in its fullness all the time, whole and complete. That which prevents men seeing it is their almost total concentration on lesser matters: their self-centred, self-satisfied absorption in that which affects physical well-being, rather than on that which will expand human consciousness.

A major task is to bring to an end the period of intense preoccupation with oneself, one's service, one's reaction to the teachings of the spirit or the promise of development. These attitudes have to be discarded and a deep sense of insecurity would do wonders in preparing for a newer and higher approach to truth. Much, if not all, of the personal problems, crises, and disasters that people experience are tests of one's capacity to lose sight of one's own goals and ambitions, and to accept responsibility for the way to respond to any stimulation to the divine plan. The standard of value for any effort is no longer that of individual progress, but is the enfoldment of group growth, and the groupings that we belong to.

Understanding does not come as a sudden illumination. It is a slow continuous growth. The next step ahead is always in the untried and the unknown. This is as true for a master soul as it is for an infant soul on the first steps of the path. There are many today that, facing the unknown, seek help and guidance with mixed motives as they try to bridge that gap between a higher and lower mind. The field of effort is so vast, so awe-inspiring as to abash humanity. Yet these are discoverable avenues of possible activity, which reveal themselves when humility changes human attitudes from personalised certainties to a spirit enquiry. As the perception of what is occurring increases, the mind becomes an instrument of spirit and demonstrates the merging of the unreal with the real. Awareness increases as attention is turned to divine wisdom, and it becomes apparent that present achievements are but keys in the opening of doors, which lead to larger experiences. The task of everybody, everywhere, is to generate the concept of the spirit idea in humanity. This is the message, which has to be given at this time. The responsibility lies in the work we put in to achieve this end.

49.   RESPONSIBILITY

Men clamour and shout in support of their rights. They protest and strike for the rights of groups, and they plunge into wars for the rights of nations. The tumult rages so fiercely that the other side of the coin is overlooked. This forgotten " other side" of "rights" is responsibility. Responsibility is the ignored factor in mankind's grasp for rights. Yet responsibility is one of the marks of the Master Soul, and the sense of responsibility is a sure sign that the spirit within is beginning to take a hold over the affairs of man on earth.

Responsibility grows from expanding experience. We shoulder responsibilities as life widens our experiences: from the first responsibility to our families into ever widening groups of business and communities, ever taking in more and more till man begins to think of his responsibilities to the spirit behind all things, and ultimately his responsibility to God.

This all comes about according to how man reacts to the vibratory quality of the divine spark, which dwells within each human being. This response is a recognition of an inner compulsion, which moves us through our daily lives in increasing complexities, until finally we begin to respond to that which we call the "Will of God". This last and highest responsibility means that we have to be trained and fit to receive and be trusted with the work of God our Father. This idea then transforms responsibility, changing it from a leaden duty to a golden opportunity showing us that our responsibilities increase as our knowledge of the laws of the spirit increases.

This carries the consequence that in increased teachings we acquire the responsibility of presenting these teachings to others. It is not a matter of re-stating what we have learned from others, but the teaching has to be presented in such a manner that it invites attention and investigation, for it is not a responsibility to compel others to accept what is truth to us, but a responsibility to make sure that the truth be seen in our thoughts, words and deeds, to the end that others may find the way less dark because of the light that filters through us.

This calls for subtle, simple, and imaginative use of our knowledge, but more and more it calls for the deepening of our spiritual experience. Here lie our gravest responsibilities, for it is useless to gain a great deal of knowledge if that knowledge does not change our lives and outlook. Our changed life and outlook then become the beacon light which others can follow. This is the responsibility of "Being"as against all the earlier responsibilities of "Doing".

Read responsibility as response-ability. The ability to respond.

50.   AS LITTLE CHILDREN

The student of the spiritual life is constantly faced with the danger of becoming lost in a maze of technicalities and details which would make the understanding on concrete mental levels a goal, rather than the discovery of the inner feelings of the spirit. Any seeker for the inner truths must learn to find that tool which can weave the twisted threads of detail knowledge into a beautiful pattern of life, and surely that tool is to be found in simplicity. It has been truly said that great minds simplify, while little minds merely complicate.

It was of simplicity that Jesus spoke when he said, "Verily I say unto you whosoever shall not receive the Kingdom of God as a little child shall in no wise enter therein". (Luke 18-17) This statement has usually been interpreted to mean that we must enter the Kingdom by means of blind faith alone, based on emotional devotion without any exercise of basic reasoning. Surely we cannot take any dogmatic position one way or the other. If we look at Christ's statement of "Being as a child" as we look at his other parables, we see that Christ was speaking not only about children, but about all of us who are the little ones spiritually speaking. He said "whosoever should humble himself as this little child, the same is the greatest in the kingdom of heaven". Simplicity and humility: these are the requirements to approach the learning of the laws of God. Yet these qualities may be applied equally as well to developing mental minds as to blind emotional acceptance. In the past, blind emotional acceptance has been tried and found wanting. Today, the power of the mind is taking centre stage for those searching to understand. Should we be saying that the main object of our lives is to become aware of the spirit behind all things, and to live and work as souls? We are called to pass beyond the intellect and into a spiritual discernment of feeling throughout our whole being: A basic instinct of the spirit. Here, because we do not depend upon logical reasoning, we find the simplicity, which shows itself as wisdom being expressed through daily lives.

This new age into which we are all entering may be described as a time when nothing is found to be impossible. So, in facing the future we need not only all the knowledge which we can command, but also to regain that sense of wonder which is the characteristic of little children. In this simplicity, humility and wonderment, let us search the laws of God, for thus we may be able to view the panorama of events, which occur daily and evaluate them without trying to settle anything permanently. We are ever faced with having to resolve complexity into a simplicity which is constantly changing. Yet the whole thing can be reduced to one simplicity: the recognition that the one life of God our Father manifests through a multitude of forms. When science discovers that there is intelligence in every atom and in every being, visible and invisible, then who can say that anything is impossible?

51.   RELIGIOUS INTEREST

The present interest in things religious creates an obvious need for guidance for those trying to distinguish between true teachings, and those meddling on the surface. One of the real benefits emerging from the chaos and confusion of today's world is the growing realisation that mankind has tended for ages to live too much on the surface of life and to ignore the deeper values.

Although orthodox religion seems to have crystallised in old age, attitudes and practices which seem out of touch with the present world and its needs, there have always been sources of direct spiritual inspiration available to men, with avenues of approach to the spiritual life open to them. These approaches change as men evolve and grow and their needs change, but the basic spiritual principles persist.

In distant times past these principles have been handed down by word of mouth and direct instruction from a teacher to a pupil. Today, the golden thread of spiritual truths is emerging in a more evident and more recognisable way to serve the demands of a 21st century humanity. The secrecy and mystery which have surrounded the basic teachings for ages are melting away. Mankind needs protection from too much stimulation during this period of infancy, and the spiritual teaching requires protection from misuse due to the ignorance of selfish and greedy humanity. However, with the experience of centuries and the lessening of ignorance, mankind is approaching that condition where increasing numbers can usefully receive the knowledge of the spiritual side of life and of himself.

Emphasis in the past has been towards the spirit through the material forces hidden in the human being, chiefly developing those psychic powers which mankind shares in common with animals. Character-building and devotion have been the high goals achieved. Today the emphasis is going deeper into the spirit, and aims more at a fusion of the spirit powers with the physical, and towards the knowledge that neither the physical, emotional nor mental spheres are the major spheres of activity; they are only fields in which the spirit serves. You serve by registering impressions, and by recognising the influence of the spirit behind all things. That means that any true spirit-centre of teaching is a group medium, through which the individual life forces become one with the spirit - a spirit that does not demand meek acceptance, but does demand activity, that will automatically bring about the separation of the good and high values from the undesirable and demeaning.

This truth in the final analysis is what we must all seek ardently. At the end of this effort, humanity will arrive at the completion which the apostle Paul promised to the Ephesians:" Then you will be filled in until you return in the plenitude of God".

52. THE TRANSFIGURATION

When considering the story of "the transfiguration" it is necessary to realise that it was not simply God revealing himself in His radiance and glory, but it also showed the medium that reveals the glory of God: the physical nature of man. In this experience we see the glorification of the physical when it expresses the divine. When we come to regard our physical bodies as the means whereby the divine can be revealed, we shall gain a new vision of physical living, and a proper incentive to cherish the bodies in which we temporally function.

Under the impact of the urging of the spark within us, we move slowly towards this recognition. Purification is the word generally used to convey the process whereby God's purpose for the physical life is revealed. The daily effort to live and meet the eventualities of human existence brings man to the point where the purification is not simply the result of life itself, but is something which is definitely imposed upon man within his own nature. It is then that we pass from just purifying ourselves to that deeper experience of our desires, feelings, pains and pleasures into their more spiritual correspondences. The mind then turns into a reflective agent of the spirit, as it turns in with a greater accuracy to the mind of the Father God. All this must, and does, effect the very structure of the physical body. It was this process carried out in the physical nature to its fullest, which led to the revelation to the Apostles of the basic nature of the Master they loved and followed.

The Transfiguration scene was the meeting-ground of great moment. Seldom does such a moment come. Usually we see only a faint glance of a possibility and of an underlying reality. We know God exists, but life with its stresses and strains so preoccupies us that we have no time to climb the mountain of vision. Let us give thanks for the life of Christ for giving us so clear a vision, and ask ourselves what are the gifts that each one of us can bring to the world, as we study the life of the Christ. We can stand as beacon lights pointing the way to the spirit behind all things, and express in daily living some of the qualities of God which Christ so perfectly portrayed, and which enabled Him to show on that Mount of Configuration the triumph of the physical being.

53. REVELATION

All life seems to be a series of awakenings, and the words "progress", "awakening", "expansion", "enlightenment" or "growth" are but a few of those applied in describing the effects of this process. What is this process but the working out of God's purpose? And God's purpose is fully known only in what we call the universal mind.

As we try to understand some fraction of this universal mind, do we look for sudden blazes of light, or do we expect it to be a gradual and progressive understanding? As we learn through experience, revelation seldom breaks in all its completed beauty into the consciousness of a person, but comes as a gradual, steady unfolding from within, and as such, life is full of revelations, recognised or unrecognised. It might be said that there is little else, for revelation is the revealing of that which is ever present. You discover or discern something more than you knew or recognised before, and you are only discovering something that has always been there. The limitation has been in one's-self. The way of revelation is through searching and discarding one's own personal or individual limitations.

Revelation can be a pictorial symbol; it can be expressed in words or come as an unvoiced recognition. It can be a sensing of a future possibility. It can also be an incentive or strong impulse in one's life. All this is because it is not something distant but a real part of one's spiritual makeup. We see that all life is a constant registration of knowledge, and in essence a learning of the things of the spirit. It is the becoming aware and the discernment of things beyond so called rational explanations. It is the becoming aware in order that daily experience can become the round for further expansions into the growth and awakening of the spirit. Bear in mind that in considering daily experiences which bring something learned, some revelation in eternal truth, one is in fact drawing in those forces that will go with this newer understanding; this is so because you need them at this point of one's life in order to move forward into a greater spiritual culture, and out of the relative darkness in which one moves at present. This, of course explains that all things one experiences have a potential for good ,which is what one would expect of all things that have their being in God.

Let us then try to keep all our thinking on revelations, with its attendant aspirations in the realms of human possibilities. We have to learn to realise the significance of any lessons being learned through our daily experiences, and know those activities which will draw out of us the greatest good. On the level of daily living, so many people are aware of impressions received but fail to recognise or use the force of the impression into some needed action. Others do react, but fail to register the true meaning which was intended. The whole theme of revelation is really one of light. It concerns the discovery of lighted areas of being which would otherwise remain unknown, and therefore within us, we are creating that light to reveal what is in the dark. This is the reality of the expression "The Light of Knowledge and of Love". Let us then reveal this light into our world. This is our responsibility.

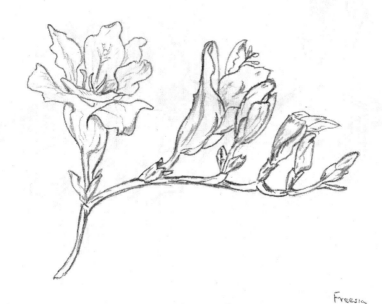

Freesia

54.   GROUP CONSCIOUSNESS

In considering the trends of thought in the world today, we find an increasing emphasis being laid upon what we would term a 'group consciousness' No longer is man living in the interests of himself alone, but he is beginning to realise the need for adjusting to the conditions of his neighbours.   He is seeing in reality that progress, contentment, peace of mind and prosperity does not exist for him alone and separated from that of his brother. This realisation is steadily expanding from the individual to the nation and thence to the family of nations. The necessity of giving instead of receiving is growing in national minds. This is showing as a sense of responsibility, and is one of the first signs that the soul is beginning to control the lives of men. Thus man is on the verge of establishing his divinity and demonstrating the life of spirit on earth.

This demonstration is very dependent upon the ability to grasp the spiritual meaning behind all events, and to transmute the lessons of the spirit in a practical knowledge whereby they may become a living experience.   It is here that we find the value of study groups, where, in a group meditation of prayer and service, our thoughts vibrate to the measure of our higher selves, and in time that vibration will become permanent.

Those who, with open eyes, enter into these services need to count the cost: the capacity to stand alone, to assume responsibility and to carry on for the sake of the achieved - all leading to that greater rapidity of vibration which demonstrates an increasing sensitiveness. This sensitiveness works out as that awareness to the inner voice of the soul. Now when a man listens to the voice of his soul, there must come an in pouring of light with its attendant problems. "How can this be" you might ask. To illustrate: - the light of the soul not only brings knowledge of God, but it also reveals how far mankind has to go on the road of divinity. The dark becomes more apparent. The chaos, the misery, and the failures stand revealed. Can one stand the pressure? Can we become acquainted with grief and yet rejoice forever in the divine consciousness, sure of the ultimate triumph of good? It is a platitude as well as a paradox to say that in the midst of distress the joy of the soul may be known and felt.   Such, however, is the case and it is for this that we must aim. Some people are happy because they shut their eyes to the truth. But students of the spirit life have their eyes wide open and are awake and alive in the spirit sense: sensitive to others and learning to live as souls.

Those who watch and guide on the inner side of life realise more than perhaps those who bear the burden and heat of physical existence, the weaknesses to be overcome. They watch with tenderness all that struggle, work, fail, continue and still serve. Not one hour of service given, not one day's labour is allowed to pass unnoticed. Take comfort in the assurance that love rules all. Take courage from the realisation that great masters protect and ever guide one nearer to our father God. That sense of immortality and the surety of an eternal future with the innate belief in God are not the prerogatives of the saints and the high ones. It is found (and sometimes in its purest form) in the humblest of people. Words of wise counsel are sounded from the lips of the illiterate and the knowledge of God in the hearts of the most unlikely.

55.   ALL LIFE IS CYCLIC IN NATURE

There is an ebb and flow in all of us and the tides are a wonderful picture of this eternal law. As we adjust ourselves to the tides of life, we begin to realise there is ever a flowing in followed by a flowing out. It can be seen over the entire process of a person's life. Some lives can be seen as apparently static and uneventful, whilst others are vibrant and full of growth and experience. This should be remembered when we are seeking to help others to live rightly. Are they passing through a period of quiet, in preparation for greater effort, or are they being subjected to an intense flow of spiritual forces? One will need strengthening and stabilising, while the other will need guidance in the direction that will produce a full and fruitful life of service.

The essential cycle for every soul is that of being born on earth, and the returning to that centre from whence it came. Some souls come to seek experience to the full, and therefore their attention is towards things physical. Others come to seek understanding from experience and they tend to retreat inwards in their outlook. Psychologists have sensed these cycles and called certain types 'extroverts' and others 'introverts'. As one grows spiritually, we find these cyclic impulses alternate with distressing rapidity. The hill and valley experience is one way of expressing this ebb and flow. Sometimes we walk in sunshine and at other times we are in the dark. Our service is on occasion fruitful and satisfying, while at other times it is arid and apparently without results. All true seekers after truth are aware of this unstable experience and frequently regard it as undesirable and to be strenuously fought. But this is the time to appreciate that the midway spot, which is neither one nor the other, provides the position on which we make our stand. This is a symbolic way of saying that we need to realise that the state of our emotions and feelings is no indication of the state of our inner spirit. We have to centre ourselves in the spirit of all things, and refuse to be influenced by surrounding conditions. Once we grasp the fact that we are experiencing the effects of the ebb and flow of the spirit life, then we must realise that it is we who are failing to respond, and are re-acting with an unevenness that is showing itself in distressing experiences. Learn that the physical side of life is simply one's field of service, and so be concerned with reacting to a rhythm that will carry, naturally and unforced, into right action and right control.

The true spiritual man seeks only the furthering of God's plan and to identify himself with the divine mind in nature. Withdrawing to the midway spot, he tries to realise his divinity, and assert that fact of his divinity through a temporary identification with the physical body of sensory perception, with all the emotions which carry the love of God to all forms of life. May there be a full and steady play of this ebb and flow of life from the spirit in all things and upon each one of us that will call forth light, love and service!   Teachers of the inner life have much to contend with as they try to influence us all. Confidence and trust will set up the right vibrations. Lack of faith, of calmness, and of application does hinder. Long patience is needed by those dealing with all that must, for lack of better material, be used. Some physical handicap may make the body non-receptive. Some worry may cause the emotional body to vibrate at a rhythm impossible for the reception of a higher purpose. Some prejudice, some criticism, some pride may make the mental body of little use. So much work is to be done! The calling within ourselves is to watch with care and keep the inner serenity, peace and mental pliability that can be used in the guarding and guiding of all mankind together in that unity of the spirit.

56.   "TO THOSE WHO GIVE ALL, ALL IS GIVEN"

There is a great law, which can be embodied in the words, "To those who give all, all is given". Most people today do not realise how true this law is, and so they do not give freely and fully to the work of spirit, or to those who have some need. Until they do, they limit their effectiveness and shut the door on supply, not only for themselves, but also for those around them with whom they are called to live. Herein lies responsibility. The way to receive is the way of being harmless to all those people with whom one is in contact in daily living; also in being harmless to those who come from the world of the spirit to serve, not just you, but the world through you. When you try to live harmlessly in thought, word and deed, and when nothing is held back materially, emotionally or from the angle of time, when strength is given with joyfulness, then you will find you will have all that is needed to carry on the work. Such is the law.

What is this work? Surely it is to provide a working, intelligent and consecrated group of servers, through whom the higher ones in spirit can carry forward and demonstrate upon the physical globe a power of spiritual energy. It is our task to call forth such a depth of consecrated love and a realisation of the opportunities, that the personality aspect of our lives will fade out from the mind, and the main preoccupation will be, "What must my service be at this time? What things in my life are not really essential, and to which I shall pay little or no attention?" These kinds of questions must be met with a balanced, intelligent and non-fanatical answer.

As we meet regularly, we gain confidence in the depths of our aspirations and desires to do good, but often the question of our courage has to be encountered, for it takes courage to make spiritual decisions and to abide by them. It takes courage to adjust our lives to the needs of the hour. It takes courage to demonstrate to those around that we care about the things of the spirit. It takes courage to deal with physical bodies as if they were free from weaknesses and tiredness, and all those handicaps which limit one: the nervousness and strains of life. It takes courage to attack life on behalf of others, forgetting our own wishes. Excuses for non-service or part-service are easily found and condoned on the basis of health, time, home limitations, age or fear of one kind or other.

Let it be repeated, " To those who give all, all is given". Take yourself as you are now, with your present equipment and in your present circumstance, and then proceed to subordinate yourself, your affairs and time, to the needs of the spirit. This is the principle calling of the situation where we stand today. May we respond to this call!

57.   TOWARDS A NEW AGE

Evidence of the end and the beginning of a new age are all around. There has been and continues to be a breakdown in many of the accustomed ways of life. Ferment due to change and the need to change has permeated the whole atmosphere of human attitudes and actions everywhere in the world. At such a time of major transition this is unavoidable, for the spiritual consciousness of men and women is not sufficiently awakened to permit a conscious, willing act of all-round co-operation for the good of the whole. People therefore pull in different directions according to their own best interests as they see fit, so adding to the physical chaos, emotional confusion and mental conflict.

All this is the effect of a tremendous spiritual stimulation as the impact of a new age and the effect of Christ's life have made on the inner climate of men's minds and hearts. There are three vast expansions of consciousness occurring at the same time within mankind at present. These indicate spiritual growth, and the necessity for men and women to achieve a broader and deeper view of life.

These three expansions in consciousness are, firstly, the realisation of the love of Christ for all mankind being born in the hearts of the people of the world as a whole. Secondly, there are those smaller groups who are willingly entering into the mainstream of Christ's redeeming work, which is God's plan for mankind. Thirdly, there are still smaller groups who are producing a completely transformed way of life, in that they are taking their physical, emotional and mental makeup and placing them under the complete control of the spiritual life.

All this is forcing people everywhere to change their sense of values and ways of thinking, and of course as these new attitudes develop, they will show themselves in physical changes as far as the concerns of men will be. Throughout the past ages humanity has learned to control and develop the substance of the world, and the results have been largely directed towards the group or national interests. Now mankind is learning to handle the material resources of the planet according to the needs of the peoples of the world and in integration with the kingdom of nature. This will demand an increased response as to the spiritual values and a change in the nature of men's desires, thus ushering in a new age of the spirit.

See 12. Religion of the New Age.

58.   DEATH   (2)

All severing of established links produce quite severe reactions in most people. Yet if it could be realised, the severing of the outer physical shell is the least severe, and the most impermanent of all such events. Failure to survive is a basic fear of most men and women, and yet it is the commonest phenomenon upon the planet. The human fear of death is primarily caused because the outlook of humanity, generally speaking, has been towards the physical expression and towards the very necessity of seeking experience through the school of earth. The number of people whose outlook on life is turned away from this is relatively so small that it truly might be stated that the fear of death remains dominate in the world.

Mankind, however, is on the eve of seeing a complete change in this condition, owing to the fact there is an increasing number of men and women who are questioning the values by which they are living. This is attracting so many in spirit, that it is creating a mounting pressure on the general 'thought atmosphere' of the globe. This will perforce bring in a new attitude towards death when it will be regarded as a natural and desirable process.

The aim of each life should be the carrying out of a definite purpose, which was known before one chose to come onto this earth. This purpose is the gaining of certain experiences recognised as necessary for the growth of spirit, and the finishing or continuing of what had begun in previous lives. When this purpose is achieved, the indwelling spirit will turn its attention elsewhere, and the outer body, having served its need, will be vacated. This, when properly understood, will lead to a life of dignity, and offers an aim worthy of our best efforts. Can we not picture the time when death, clearly recognised and welcomed by man, could be described by him in the phrase, "The time has come when my spirit requires that I relinquish my body and restore it to the place from whence it came"? Imagine the change in outlook of mankind when death comes, to be regarded as an act of giving up a form, which had been temporarily taken in order to gain experience in the physical world, thereby taking the opportunity to reach a higher point of perfection on life's way.

To so many people death comes as an unexpected and sadly anticipated event. Yet it is a true soul activity, talking of death as it comes through disease or old age, and not through accident or some war activities. It is factual in nature, unavoidable in practice and as familiar as any of those activities that govern all life on earth.

59. TO BE A STUDENT

Many students of the spirit today register or sense an impression under special circumstances, but few as yet have achieved a degree of synthesis through which they can formulate their own approach to the laws of spirit with any degree of certainty. There are two main reasons for this: (1) the present approach to spiritual training on a large scale is new on this earth and in its pioneer stage. (2) No clear basic correlation has yet been attempted between the modern social system and the spiritual teachings of man that are seeping through all levels of human consciousness. Thus, there is a wide gap between the schools of spiritual teachings and the academic, scientific and religious institutions. When these correlations are finally made, as they will be by incoming generations, the world of spirit will have available new and better channels for a closer approach to a confused and disillusioned humanity. Meanwhile, it is part of our function to prepare for this great development. In this preparatory work we need to know exactly why contemporary social sciences cannot as yet conceive, or be aware of the spirit behind all things. In any teaching, writing and meditation, it is essential to gather together all the ideas and concepts prevalent with the social thinking of the times, bearing in mind that social sciences are focused around man as he is known physically, biologically, psychologically self-focused and personalised. These sciences are circumscribed by a sense of identity and surrounded by a frame of reference, which is merely dense matter. Spirit cannot possibly enter into these narrow and specialised areas of learning while they remain focused as such. Thus religion and education today have no sound basis for an approach to man's large and greater destiny in the cosmic spiritual order.

Hence it happens that today the thinking limitations of personal existence are rarely discussed, or even imagined in educational and religious circles. Like the weather, they are taken for granted in the belief that nothing can be done about them, and as a result, no organised effort has as yet been made to formulate the laws of the spirit of man, or to link them with the many forms of expression through which the spirit does manifest itself. Genius itself is nothing but a fragmentary expression of spirit bursting through the confining walls of sensory forms. Thus we are called to demonstrate vision and leadership with the confidence of a future life that will be of the fullness of the spirit.

60. SOUL (1)

The soul is that factor which emerges out of the contact between spirit and matter which produces a sensitive response and which we call consciousness in its varying forms. It is also that latent quality which makes itself felt as light or human radiation. Matter per se in its undifferentiated state, prior to being swept into activity through the creative process is NOT POSSESSED of soul, and therefore does not possess the qualities of response and radiation. Only when spirit and matter are brought into conjunction and fusion does the soul appear giving to these two aspects of divinity the opportunity to manifest and the chance to demonstrate salient activity and magnetic radiatory light.

The soul of all things is the "Anima mundi" as it expresses itself through the four kingdoms in nature and is that which gives our planet its light. The 'planetary light' is the sum total of the light to be found in all atoms of radiatory and vibratory matter composing all forms in all kingdoms. There is within the planet and within each kingdom in nature the etheric body underlying the outer physical form and man's etheric body is a corporate part of the planetary etheric body constituting its most refined and highly developed aspect.

The soul is light literally from the vibratory angle, and philosophically from the angle of being the true medium of knowledge, for it throws its light into the brain which is like an eye looking out into the physical world. The brain is responsive to seven senses through which contact with the world of matter and spirit becomes possible: hearing - touch -sight - taste -smell- the mind as the common sense - and the intuition as the synthetic sense. The intuition is literally the immediate grasp of the truth as it essentially exists The vague word "consciousness" could be superseded by the word "awareness". In varying degrees man is aware. His response apparatus responds to and is influenced by all the contacts made. But to be "intuitionally aware" he must be capable of reacting, not only to external stimuli but to contacts emanating from within himself, and also from the worlds of introspection and of mystical vision which seem sealed to all subhuman forms of life. When man has learned to see below the surface and has cultivated true vision, then we shall have the steady emergence of the quality of the soul in all forms. It is this world of meaning which is the privilege of humanity to reveal and all true searchers of truth should be pioneers in the field.

The spirit (man's emanating source of energy) begins to use the soul via the intuition, and to impress upon the soul consciousness those laws, knowledge, forces and inspirations which will make the soul the instrument of the spirit. As the soul assumes control, via the mind, so the brain becomes responsive to the soul. One of the first lessons we need to learn is that our minds, being as yet unresponsive to the hidden intuitions, makes it impossible for us to say with assurance that such a condition is this, that, or the other. Until we aim to function in our soul consciousness, it is not for us to say what is or what is not.

Rose

60a.   SOUL (2)

The soul is that factor in matter, or rather that which emerges out of contact between spirit and matter, which produces a sensitive response and what we call consciousness in its varying forms. It is also that latent quality which makes itself felt as light or luminous radiation. Matter in its undifferentiated state prior to being swept into activity through the creative process is not possessed of soul, and therefore does not possess the qualities of response and radiation. Only when in the creative and evolutionary process when the spirit is brought into conjunction with matter does the soul appear, and give to these two aspects the chance to demonstrate sensitivity and magnetic light. The soul, therefore, may be regarded as that unified sensitivity and relative awareness of that which lies at the back of all forms.   The soul is that principle of sensitiveness underlying all outer manifestation. When the soul is simply sensitivity, it produces quality and a capacity to react to vibration and to environment as the kingdoms of nature. When the soul adds the capacity of detached self-awareness, there appears that self-identified entity which we call a human being.

When the soul adds to its sensitivity and self-awareness, the consciousness of the group, then there appears the initiate and the master. When the soul adds to its sensitivity, self-awareness and group consciousness, a consciousness of divine synthetic purpose (called by us The Plan), then we have that state of being which is distinctive of all those upon the Path, the great advanced beings from the Masters to the life of the planets themselves. Forget not that when we make these distinctions, it is nevertheless our soul that is functioning, acting through varyingly refined bodies of different capacities. So we see that the soul is that entity, which is brought into being when the spirit aspect and the matter aspect are related to each other. The soul, therefore, is neither spirit nor matter, but is the relation between them.

The soul is the form-building aspect, which drives all God's creatures forward along the path of evolution. The soul is the force of evolution itself. The soul plays upon matter forcing it to assume certain shapes; to respond to certain vibrations, and to build those specified phenomenal forms which we recognise in the physical world as mineral, vegetable, animal and human. The qualities, vibrations, colours and characteristics in all kingdoms of nature are soul qualities. Qualities are brought into being through the interplay of the pairs of opposites, spirit and matter, and their effect upon each other. This is the basis of that which we call consciousness. Therefore the soul might be defined as that which feels, registers awareness, attracts and repels, responds or denies response, and keeps all forms in a constant vibratory activity.

The soul is, however, limited in its expression by the nature and quality of the form in which it is found, and there are consequently forms which are highly

responsive to and expressive of the soul, and others which are incapable of recognising the higher aspects of soul.
The soul can be known as a 'triplicity':-

1) The Spiritual Will: that quota of the universal will which any one soul can express, and which is adequate for the purpose of enabling a man to co-operate in the purpose of the great life in which he has his being.

2) Spiritual Love: The quality of group consciousness of inclusiveness, of mediatorship, of attraction or of unification. This is the paramount characteristic, for only the soul has it as the dynamic factor. It is that dominating force of soul life where the soul can be en rapport with all souls.

3) The Body Nature: While the spirit is primarily the expression of will, with love and intelligence, the body nature is distinguished by intelligence. When the intelligence of the body nature is fused with the love of the soul, then wisdom is demonstrated. When the soul has infolded all its powers and learned to include within its consciousness all that is, then in turn a higher or more inclusive state becomes possible, and soul life is superseded by monadic life.

Matter is the vehicle for the manifestation of soul on this plane of existence , and soul is the vehicle on a higher plane for the manifestations of spirit, and these three are trinity.

61. THE CHRIST

What is meant by "The Christ"? The word Christ is derived from the Greek word "Kristos" and means anointed. It is identical with the Hebrew word "Messiah". The word Christ, per se, does not refer to any particular person. Every anointed person is Christed. When the definite article "the" is placed before the word Christ, a definite personality is indicated and this personality is none other than a member of the Trinity: - The Son. This son is Love. So the Christ is Love, and Love is God.

Jesus was the name of the man, and it was the only appropriate name, for the word means "Saviour" and Jesus was in many senses a saviour. The word Christ was his official title, as it means "The Master of Love". When we say "Jesus the Christ" we refer to the man and to his office just as we do when we say "George the King" or "Lincoln the President". George was not always King, and Lincoln was not always President. So Jesus was not always Christ. Jesus won his Christship by a strenuous and dedicated life. Jesus was a man and Christ was the God-man. This is the pattern for mankind to follow. In this realisation we grow into the Spirit and play our part in redeeming the world.

"No man has ever been saved by theology, but only by the awakened consciousness of the Christ within each heart"

Alice Bailey

62.   THE RETURN OF THE CHRIST

The idea of the return of the Christ is a most familiar one. Ever since He apparently departed, groups of people have reasoned among themselves into the belief that on such and such a date He will come back, and ever the expectations have been doomed to failure. He has not come, and such people have been laughed at. Their eyes have not seen Him and there has been no tangible indication of His presence.

The truth is that Christ cannot return because He has always been here upon the earth watching over the spiritual destiny of mankind. He has always guided the affairs of those workers who have had the well being of all mankind in their hearts. He may not be able to be seen, but He can be recognised. Seeing and recognising are two very different things. We will not recognise Him as the result of any proclamation or any great event, which would force human beings everywhere to say "Lo; He is here for here are the signs of His divinity". We should recognise the increasing stimulation of the spiritual consciousness in men and women everywhere as a result of the spirit of Christ drawing nearer to the hearts of the people. This is happening with most effective results, hence the increasing demands of people of goodwill for what is called in these early stages 'welfare movements', and the greater attention being paid to distressing conditions anywhere in the world.

As a result of the teachings of the churches these last two thousand years, Christ has been a silent, passive figure. The time has now come to get a truer picture of Christ active among the people, for in the future the eyes of humanity will be fixed upon Christ, when He will be recognised as working through his followers behind all world affairs, and this His work is very much conditioned and determined by the reactions of mankind as a whole. His work is also subject to the responses and understanding of that greater being we call our Father God. Between God and man Christ has to adjust and bring about a right timing and a turning of the many mistakes of man into good. The vision of Christ is so vast and His grasp of causes and effects, of action and reaction is such that the arriving at a right decision at the right time is a wonder to behold. Human beings are apt to look at all that happens from purely human and an immediate angle. Do they ever think of the problems and decisions which the Christ faces today?

Our task is then to develop the mind and heart of Christ within us, and to see life and events in the light of spiritual values as He does. Let us look at the problems as He sees them, then we will not just recognise His every presence, but we will be hastening that time when he will be seen again. How, where, or when is not of our concern. Our work is to do our utmost to prepare all mankind in order that He be recognised.

63. SPIRITUAL UNITY

It is easy to become confused by the idea of building and uniting to form a whole, and thinking that it is the same thing as that basic underlying unity of God and all life. The sense of spiritual unity that we all have to develop is something quite different. If we mix together all the colours in a paint box we might make indigo, but we cannot achieve the colour, or non-colour, of white. Yet white holds within it all the other colours. There lies the difference. White is not something we can make, but it is something we can recognise. White is the true underlying unity of all the colours.

The tendency to try and unite all people in the world is very apparent today, as people are grasping more fully the idea that there is only one world, and one humanity in the mind of God. Yet we must realise that the required one-ness is not a unity of people, nor a single world religion, but it is a fellowship of the spirit which is required. One humanity is required in the sense of a common shared humanness rather than a body of like-minded people. It is a unity of life and not a unity of bodies. This life, this inner spirit will express it-self in many ways, as each human unit is unique in its own way. There can be unity and diversity, but there is also something that supports both, which is so difficult to put into words, and which can only be described as of the very essence of God.

How do you develop this sense of underlying unity? Firstly, by recognising that every attempt to unify and bring together into a harmony is a help and a step in the right direction, but not sufficient by itself. Without a spiritual identifi-cation with the whole, these attempts do not go far enough. To bring about a spiritual identification with the whole, we have to build a bridge to the world of spirit values. This can be done in places of prayer where people may meet regularly in meditative study, searching and trying to understand the higher values of life, while yet serving and working in the day- to- day affairs of the world. In the steady strengthening of those links between the world of spiritual values and the material world, we achieve an ever-increasing sensitivity to higher impressions and so to inner inspiration. Recognising the workings of the spirit within is recognising that which binds all life together.

To spur us on to attain the needed effort, let us recognise that the result of this attainment is the life more abundant that the Christ spoke of. In older church terms, a heavenly bliss, which can be accepted by each one of us as an inner feeling of well being.

64.   CHRIST IN YOU; THE HOPE OF GLORY

Today we stand at the verge of the birth of the Christ in all men.   For it was not simply the birth of the divine teacher, but also the appearance of one who not only summed up in himself all the past achievements of mankind, but who was also the forerunner of the future, in that he embodied in himself all that was possible for humanity to achieve.   The history of mankind is the history of individual search for divine expression, and the achievement of a new birth which releases a man into service of the kingdom of God.   Always, the germ of the living Christ has been present, though hidden, in every human being and in due time the infant soul makes its appearance.   That kingdom exists and birth into it is as inescapable as birth into a human family.   Through birth, service and sacrifice one becomes a citizen of that kingdom, and this is as much a natural process connected with the spiritual life as are the physical processes in one's outer life.   These two go together.

The way into the kingdom is found by questioning and answering, by seeking and finding, and by obedience to that inner voice which can be heard when all other voices are stilled.   There comes a point of spiritual development when one is sufficiently sensitive to the influence of the divine, to be aware of what may be called "God's Will" expressing itself through a voice within.   When that prompting is heard, we become aware of the possibilities of God within ourselves.   Then it is that we realise in ourselves the outpouring of divine love which makes us see that we are one with all other lives.   It is then that we find and meet the Christ within.   Would not this voice within indicate then, as did the historical Christ, the way that must be trodden, the way that leads away from the superficial and the material, into the world of inner reality?   In the bible story, Christ showed us in himself, and his life, what a man should be: ever obedient to the highest that is in us, sharing love to all beings, with complete confidence in the power of God to demonstrate the life of loving service, and living as sons of God in the setting which destiny has placed us, there being nowhere else possible at this time and day. We have in our present lives, if we could but realise it, exactly those circumstances and the environment in which the great lesson of obedience to the highest provides the tests to try our strength and reveal where our weaknesses lie.   God has need of men and women thus tested, so that they will not break, or waver, when difficulties come in the life of service, which is the next great step towards demonstrating the life of the Christ within.   He left us the example, and we must carry on the work which he began.

Now it is no good studying the life of Christ from a distance, wondering at his achievements or trying to copy him. We would venture to say that he does not want to be copied, but he wants us to prove to ourselves and to the world that the divinity, which is in him, is in us also. What can we do to respond to this call of holiness?
First it entails effort - the will to overcome the lower nature and to listen to the

insistent demand of the spirit within. This calls forth recognition of that presence of the spirit, which can be known through the process of daily living. Secondly, it calls for the determination to achieve a refocusing of one's entire nature into a closer identification with the spirit. From this, we begin to assume a right attitude to life, and to see what must be done. How can this truth of the spirit be experienced simply and practically so that its meaning can appear, thus enabling us to do what is needed in life? Perhaps when we truly know that hidden in every human being is the son of God who is the Christ in us, the hope of glory. As yet this may be only a hope, but as the wheels of life carry us from one lesson to another, we approach nearer and nearer to the indwelling reality, and in due time the long journey draws to a close and the hidden Christ is born. Is this not what character is all about?

65. THE SICKNESS OF THE SOUL

The sickness of the soul in modern man is a very good thing, for it is a healing fever. There can be no shadows without light, and if the shadows in your world of today seem black and brooding, it is because you have the moral light by which to see them.

And so you see a great deal of evil in the world, not because the evil is newly come to the world, but because you have a new way of looking at it. Powerful new search-lights of thought turn into the dark corners of social, moral and religious life. How do you know that so many of the conditions that exist in the world today are of evil? What is it that makes man seek new and better conditions on recognising some old and undesirable structure?

Man has sometimes called this an idealism, but what is the meaning and significance of idealism? Idealism is a result - not the cause of man's search for something better than what he has known before. For causes you must look deeper. Man is like the atom, he has within himself vast potential energy - and the cause of any idealism lies in this incredible spiritual energy within the soul of the human atom, for it is in the nature and the power of this energy to make "all things new".

As the soul force within your very being grows in strength and light, it projects images upon the screen of the mind, giving an imaginative vision in advance of the rational mind of the needs of the hour and the future. It is then, the responsibility of people of intelligence to fuse and harness this great power of the soul, that it may guide the people into the process of cleansing all that is unclean and dark. This is what mankind as a whole is now doing -- never doubt this. The confusion and destruction in the world today is the pain of this great life giving force struggling in old channels of consciousness. Above the temples of knowledge has always been the inscription "Man Know Thyself", and through countless ages, man has sought this Truth of Being.

This compulsion for growth of the soul must come from within, and the first instrument of preparation is your conscience, the "still small voice" as scriptures call it, which first separates the good from the undesirable that prevents the light of the Living God from executing its great powers of Life. As this still small voice begins to show the good from the not-so-good, you then go through the stage of Repentance - to use the Church's phrase. This is really the overwhelming desire to change, to do better, and the desire for the knowledge of God. Thus you grow in spiritual strength to a state of feeling and a sensing of the spiritual nature deeply hidden in the innermost part of one's being.   This will result in a steady process of thinking, which changes the outlook on life and transmutes base desires into nobler emotions, and you come into a realisation of knowing beyond the ordinary state and process of logic.

But to approach this state of Divine being, you must first realise that all true knowledge is soul knowledge and when you know your soul, then there are no longer the two identities of one wanting to know, and the god to be known, for both are one and instead of saying "I know God to be" ... you say, "I am." This gives the deep faith based upon knowledge - the result "of feeling by experience" which in its unswerving confidence may move mountains. Faith in action reveals the indestructible nature, origin and destiny of the human spirit. The soul- directed life transmits Divine energy to selfless service. Service is the expression of the soul.

Then we have imagination, God's great gift to his creature man. It is the handmaid of faith - producing the creative faculty of idealism, which, when guided and directed by Divine Will, has a potency beyond ordinary expressions. The universe is the product of a cosmic imagination, and man in his smaller world calls forth forms for good or evil from his imagination, to the extent that he contacts his interior world. So man becomes the thoughts he thinks: if of the light, then light will be born, and if of darkness, then chaos will result. A strong imagination can accomplish much, the radiation from which is an all-impelling force enabling him to use spiritual powers, and to understand inner realms of the Spirit, where the enduring things by which man should live are to be found. If man is to inherit the Kingdom of Heaven, he must seek that part of himself which alone contains within itself the essence of God.

Each age produces the method best suited to its day's growth in finding this essence. All through the ages God has revealed himself. Never has He left His people without witness, for always these have been men possessed with a sense beyond the threshold of the usual - possessing another worldliness, expressing in a greater beauty, love, and hope that was then manifest, and through these lives we trace mankind reaching out for a deeper knowledge of himself.

This is a long road, and a ceaseless one - and in this day and age you will wonder what can you do that you are not already doing or attempting to do - nothing startling. These ideas will not give you an insight into magic formula which will help you develop into Divine beings overnight. No, like all ideas based on the Laws of growth, they lead you to the simple rules of ever accumulating knowledge to make a seedbed for Soul growth, and above all, service with the tools you have. Through these you can intensify your efforts, without being so involved emotionally, that you fail to make the best use of your expanding knowledge, and opportunities that must come with the ever-greater growth and expanse of the Spirit. God gave man life and the power to draw to himself the life more abundantly. The door is open. Man has to reach forth and accept it.

66. PURIFICATION

Purification is of many kinds and degrees. There is physical purity, moral purity, and there is that purity that makes a man a channel of spirit forces, something we all have in differing degrees. Would you agree with us if we say the sound of the word 'purity' brings us the image of a freedom from limitation, a freedom from the imprisoning of the spiritual essence? There can be no achievement without some purity. There is no possibility of seeing or manifesting divinity without passing through the waters that cleanse, and in the world today a great cleansing is going on. An unforced abstinence from much that has hitherto been deemed desirable is going on in the world, and none can escape it. This is due to a breakdown of many systems, notably the economic system, proving ineffectual. A purification is being forced upon the people and as a consequence a true sense of values must result.   A cleansing from wrong ideas is needed. A purification from dishonest standards and undesirable objectives is being powerfully applied, and who is to say that, as all the people of the world recognise the values of this self applied purification, Christ's great ideal as he expressed in the words "Blessed are the pure in heart, for they shall see God" will indeed be seen as true and factual.

In the story of the baptism we see reference to two kinds of purification. First, that of John who baptises by water, and then of Christ's baptism of the Holy Ghost and of fire. Can we say that the purification of water is the purifying of the fluid nature of ourselves, the constant shifting between pleasure and pain, or the storms which arise in daily living and the peace and calm that can descend? John the Baptist testified that this purification must always be a preliminary step to the purification by fire. John's outer washing, symbolising an inward washing, was in truth a call to men to listen to their own conscience, for conscience calls you to recognise higher values and deeper truths. That surely is seeing God in Christ's words "They shall see God" or shall we say that when the conscience prods you to purify your heart or life, you will recognise all things as good? Now when you see all is goodness, you are indeed seeing a vision of the Kingdom of God. You are seeing that all things are coming from the spirit and are reflected in the outer world that is your world. Now you are ready for the Baptism of the Holy Ghost and fire, for fire is spirit ,and the purification of the spirit is that state when the Soul of man is in complete control of all his life, and there is no barrier to the life and purpose of the Spirit. When there are no barriers and channels are free, the vision of God's purpose and meaning becomes clear.

Become aware of your divinity, not merely as a deeply spiritual hope and a heart's desire, but to know yourself as a son or daughter of God. We see God in nature, God in Christ and God in Man. This should give you confidence and power to go forward in life, stepping with courage from the known towards the unknown. Like the story of the Christ purified by the Jordan water, you can then go and meet whatever temptation you may encounter, always standing firm in the Holy Spirit that burns within you. For remember the bible story points out to us, that though we go through the purifying process and come out cleansed, we still have to meet and overcome temptations before we can work as Sons of God, inviting others by our example to lead a life of purity in Christ -like love of all Life.

67. THERE IS NEITHER JEW NOR GENTILE: THERE IS ONLY HUMANITY

Down the ages the Jew has been wandering, producing much of beauty in the world and giving to humanity many of its greatest men. At the same time he has been hated, persecuted, betrayed and hounded.

The World War that ended in 1945 should have brought about the beginning of the end of this enmity, when there was that opportunity for a co-operative relationship on either side, and when a surge of goodwill could have begun that process of slow assimilation to break down old habits of thought and reparative customs. Surely a study of the Jewish nation down the ages is to see the pattern and symbol of all mankind. The Jew embodies in himself the history of mankind, for the Jew is the symbol of humanity.

The outstanding characteristic of the Jews is their tendency to grasp and to hold. To preserve their racial and national integrity, they have ever chosen to stand for separation, to regard themselves as the chosen people and have had an innate consciousness of high destiny. Can it not be said that that high destiny is to present to the world a symbol of ONE HUMANITY? For it must be HUMANITY which is the chosen people and not one small fraction of the race. The Jews ever present the problem of the "eternal pilgrim" wandering through the maze of Human evolution gazing with longing eyes towards the promised land, but that "eternal pilgrim" is the mass of all men, refusing to comprehend that there is a underlying spiritual purpose behind all material phenomena, the grasping for material good and steadily rejecting the things of the spirit.

If the Jewish race could recall their high symbolic destiny, if the rest of humanity would see themselves in the Jewish people, and if both groups would emphasise the fact of one human stock, and cease thinking of themselves in terms of national and racial units, the destiny of all humanity could radically change from the retributive destiny of the present to the recompensing good of the future. Regarding this question from the long-range vision (looking backward historically as well as forward hopefully) the problem is one to which the Jews themselves must make the larger contribution. They have never faced candidly and honestly, as a race, the problem of why so many nations have never liked nor wanted them. Yet there must be some reason, inherent in the people themselves when the reaction is so general and universal. Their approach to the problem has been one of supplication, of distressed complaint or of unhappy despair. Their demand has been for the Gentile nations to put the matter right and many Gentiles have attempted to do so. However, until the Jews themselves face up to the situation, and admit that there may be for them, the working out of the retributive aspect of that law of life in cause and effect, and until they endeavour to ascertain what it is in them, as a race which has initiated their ancient and dire fate, this basic world issue will   remain as it has been since the very night of time.

This in no way mitigates the guilt of those who have so sorely abused the Jews. The behaviour of the nations towards the Jews, particularly in those atrocities of the last world war, has no excuse. The situation has now assumed the form of a vicious circle of error and wrong doing, of retribution and revenge, and in view of this, the time must come when together the nations of the world must confer upon this problem, and co-operate to bring to an end the wrong attitudes of both sides.

This can only be solved by many conditions: the presentation of an accepting will, a co-operative love of humanity, a frank acknowledgement of responsibility, and a skilful adjustment of united joint activity to bring about the good of humanity as a whole, and not just the good of a individual nation or race of people. The Jewish problem will not be solved by pliant and demand, by financial manipulations nor the possession of any land.

68.   A NEW EVOLUTIONARY FORCE - MAN

By the crossing of a new step, that of reflection, man reaches the conscientiousness of: - 'He knows what he knows'. This gives him the sense of time and history, the aptitude for planning and choosing, the freedom to act and the notion of good and evil. In fact intelligence is an extraordinary force which intervenes from now on in evolution. This must bring change across the face of the earth. Man's various inventions will give him the control of life on this planet and thus will ensure his supremacy. This instinct of growth pushes him to constitute increasingly complex and interdependent social assemblies, which little by little, envelope the globe.

Intelligence intervenes strongly in the evolutionary process with the irruption of human freedom of choice and responsibility. It is a force added to the evolutionary growth. It is here that man substitutes consciousness to the blind power of instinct. Man is the actor who becomes responsible for the future of evolution. The best and the worst are possible. All technical progress generated can be regarded as tools of evolution. Our greatness consists in serving like intelligent atoms in the task that is underway in the universe. What supports our vision is the majestic magnitude of the cosmogenesis accessible to us, coherent and compatible in the structure of thought that science gives us. We have a world fulfilling itself in our reasoning, as Pope John-Paul II pointed out " Faith and reason are as two wings which make it possible for the human spirit to rise towards the contemplation of the truth". This truth is what, in the final analysis, every man must seek ardently.

The whole mass of the universe is in evolution, and man is immersed in it. Evolution follows a line towards more complexity and man seems to be the summit of that complexity. The relationship linking complexity and consciousness is man, the most highly-minded being in the Biosphere. His intelligence gives him the power to intervene in the evolutionary process. He may be considered the culmination of that process, potentially leading towards a higher level of complexity and consciousness, attracted by the transcending focus of convergence towards an omega point. Man's future is in the achievement of this extreme state of consciousness. Man forms a part of the whole and this whole is in evolution. A great question arises: Does evolution go somewhere or does it get lost in nothingness? This question commands our attitude to life. There was a beginning; there is nothing in the universe except energy in one form or another. In fact, matter is a representation of energy, both as an equivalent and as transformable one to the other. A gradually increasing complexity characterises the history of the universe in its physical aspects leading to man, whose brain is formed of myriads of interconnected cells and is the apex of the pyramid of complexity.

Psychic interiority as a result of the hyper-complexity is probably present to a differing degree in all the living, and this truth, in the final analysis, is what any man must seek ardently - at the end of which humanity will arrive at that completion which St Paul promised to the Ephesians, "Thus you will be able to understand, with all the faithful- - - - Then you will be filled until you return in the plenitude of God"

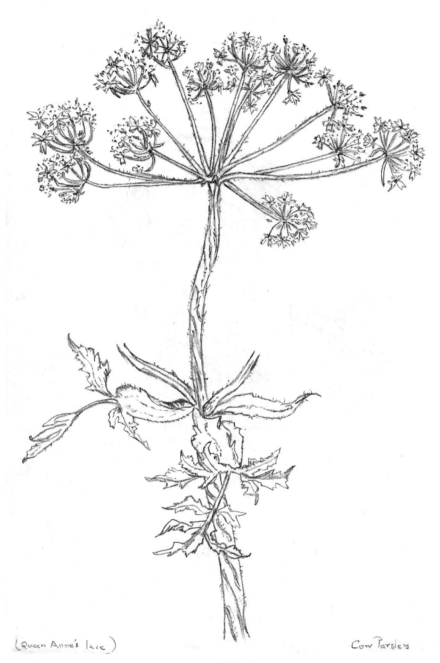

(Queen Anne's lace)   Cow Parsley